Rivals or a Team?

RIVALS *or a* TEAM?

Clergy-Musician Relationships in the Twenty-First Century

Eileen Guenther

foreword by Paul Westermeyer

MorningStar Music Publishers, Inc.
1727 Larkin Williams Road, St. Louis, MO 63026-2024
www.morningstarmusic.com

Printed in the United States of America

ISBN 978-0-944529-54-6

Library of Congress Cataloging-in-Publication Data

Guenther, Eileen Morris.
Rivals or a team : clergy-musician relationships in the twenty-first century / Eileen Guenther ; foreword by Paul Westermeyer.
p. cm.
ISBN 978-0-944529-54-6 (alk. paper)
1. Ministers of music. 2. Clergy—Office. 3. Church musicians—Vocational guidance. I. Title.
ML3001.G84 2012
264'.2—dc23
2012018282

All personal correspondence quoted in this book is reprinted with the permission of the writers.

Editorial assistance: Margaret Shannon
Cover design: Kim Jackson
Book design: Kristen Schade

This book is dedicated to

my mother, the church musician who inspired me to follow in her footsteps,

my father, who drove me to piano lessons in my youth and who,
in his last days, encouraged my writing this book,

and to Roy and Christina.

Contents

Foreword

Christopher Page in *The Christian West and its Singers: The First Thousand Years* (2010) recounts two realities which, when taken together, may seem puzzling: 1) that the church from the beginning has regarded music very highly, and 2) that it has kept musicians under surveillance. A corollary is related, that clergy rank higher than musicians. These realities become less puzzling when it is realized that music's power gives musicians idolatrous temptations that have to be kept in check. Through their calling to preach the Word and preside at the sacraments, the clergy exercise a substantial portion of that check.

This check on music and musicians, while understandable, wise, and at heart a good thing, is open to its own idolatrous temptations. It can turn into a power grid in which clergy succumb to power's perversions. One of these—in our culture often through the addictive pretensions of the empire's CEO—is to abuse musicians. Musicians, sinners just like clergy, are capable of terrible things; but systemic abuse is more characteristic of clergy who, because they possess more power, can more easily succumb to its corrupting potential.

Although Eileen Guenther recounts some of the horror stories the corrupting perversions have visited on the church, they are not the topic of this book. They serve as historical and theological backdrops. She presumes them and does not back away from their reality. But she also does not back away from positive partnerships and how to pursue them. That is her major concern. To that end she addresses the practical dimensions of how clergy and musicians may best relate to one another.

It might be assumed that there is nothing noteworthy or necessary about a book that explores how persons in the church should relate to one another. It might be assumed that, especially in the church, good relationships are obvious and automatic. Such assumptions would be as wrong as ones that see any human relationships, marriage, for example, as requiring no thought or being obvious and automatic. Guenther has brought to bear on the topic her own personal experience as a church musician and teacher, laced with the expertise of others. She approaches the topic with personal testimonies and analysis, illustrates its nuance, and provides the careful thought it deserves.

There are many things Guenther teaches us. One of these is illustrated by how often the word "respect" appears. Though striking, this is not surprising. Respect is not generated by abuse, power plays, or ego needs. It is generated instead by open, honest give and take, exhibited by competent people who understand their complementary roles and work together for the common good.

That by itself is worth knowing. Guenther teaches us something far deeper, however, namely, why respect and its corollaries are important. Two recurring themes unpack this why. One is the strength and persistence of the call church musicians experience. Guenther and the people she quotes acknowledge that there are musicians who treat church jobs as opportunities to go through musical motions and earn a little money. Some churches in their "hiring" practices even encourage this. The church musicians who are described here, however, do not fit such a mold. They have a sense of call as deep, authentic, and profound as any pastor.

Another recurring theme may be even more important. It is the amazing relationships and partnerships that some clergy and musicians have experienced. These have provided intensely rewarding vocations for the parties involved, which is no small thing all by itself. More significantly, the parties in these partnerships have provided feasts for the people they served—for the glory of God and the good of the neighbor.

May healthy partnerships increase through the work Eileen Guenther has done for us. Thanks be to God for it.

Paul Westermeyer

Acknowledgments

I would like to express my gratitude to the many clergy and musician colleagues who have shared their testimonies with me, their thinking about qualities they are looking for in their counterparts, and what their ministries mean to them. They are members of theological faculties as well as musicians and clergy serving churches in a wide range of denominations and locations. Some of the stories of the church musicians were written with great difficulty because of the excruciating pain they had experienced, and I am grateful to them for their heartfelt stories, which immeasurably enrich this book.

Likewise, deep gratitude goes to Mark Lawson of MorningStar Publishers for his invitation to write this book, and my colleagues Barbara Green, Jo Ann McClain, Lewis Parks, James Thomashower, and John Thornburg for reading the manuscript and sharing helpful suggestions. The book absolutely could not have been completed without the editorial assistance of my friend and colleague Margaret Shannon, or the insight and encouragement provided by my husband Roy Guenther. Finally, my father died as I was writing the book. As the husband of a church musician who sometimes worked with pesky clergy, Dad was very supportive of my work and the difference he hoped it would make in the church music profession. I am profoundly grateful for his love and support through the process.

Introduction

I am a church musician and the daughter of a church musician. I grew up in Baptist and Presbyterian churches and have worked in a Lutheran campus ministry and in Episcopal and United Methodist churches. I have committed my life to enabling the power of music to resound in worship, and I am thrilled to be able to share that passion at Wesley Theological Seminary as well as in places where I play or conduct workshops. I am exhilarated by the sound of enthusiastic congregational singing, and I am passionate about planning worship services with colleagues and worship teams. I delight in playing magnificent organs in wonderful spaces and conducting the major works of the sacred choral repertoire with orchestra, but I am equally inspired when I hear the robust singing of a South African congregation or the contemplative strains of a Taizé chant.

In all of the churches where I have worshiped and worked, the core of the ministry team (although some never think about it that way) is the same: the pastor and the musician—the most significant staff relationship in a church and one of the most critical components in any church's realization of its mission and ministry. With one exception, I have been blessed with excellent working relations with clergy. It still breaks my heart to hear about un-collegial, unhealthy and sometimes even abusive relationships that exist between clergy and musicians. Musicians and clergy work together as the principal leaders and designers of worship, although sometimes with different perspectives on the worship experience or on their relationship. As a consequence of these different perspectives, they are the very church staff members most likely to be in conflict. My work with the American Guild of Organists (AGO) has provided a broad frame of reference that has informed my conviction that we, the clergy-musician team, are called to new ways of communicating, dealing with conflict, and supporting each other, with the goal of serving the church more effectively.

The reality in most churches is that ultimate decision-making and power resides with the clergy, and musicians do not dispute this. There is, however, a difference between the polity of a denomination and the way that polity is carried out. This is where the conflict often resides. Musicians seldom, if ever, win in a power conflict with clergy. It is therefore no coincidence that I hear most about the unhappiness of musicians, particularly complaints of mistreatment and unfair termination from their church positions. I do not believe, however, that the problem is always only on the part of the clergy; both parties can be contributors in such conflict.

The point is not who is wrong or who is right. The point is—or should be—that we are all in this together, and it is in our best interest and the church's best interest for us to construct a framework upon which we can build a collegial relationship, a real team. In addressing this complex relationship, we cannot overlook the fact that this is a challenging time for the church. Many churches are experiencing diminishing resources and membership, adding to the stress often felt by the clergy and musicians who serve those churches. In addition, there have been frequent seismic shifts in worship style that represent one of the greatest challenges facing the church today. Thomas Long in *Beyond the Worship Wars* (2001) calls music "the nuclear reactor of congregational worship." He warns: "Change the order of worship, and you may set off a debate. Change the style of music, and you may split the congregation." Whether it is a change in worship style or a change in music, there are significant challenges facing worship leaders today. My conviction is that we—the clergy-musician team—must address these issues intentionally, prayerfully, and creatively together.

Why a book about teamwork? Why, specifically, a book about the clergy-musician team? Teamwork is widely regarded as the best, if not the only way, to build success. This book offers a look at musicians as they engage with the larger staff team, but its primary focus is the clergy-musician team, including strategies for forming effective teams, healthy ways to deal with conflict, and transition strategies for situations in which it just doesn't work out. Finally, there are testimonies from clergy and musicians that give witness to what each would have the other know. It is my prayer that this book will provide insights and inspire conversations that will change "what is" to *what can be.*

It may very well be that the future of the church is at stake.

Eileen Guenther
Vienna, Virginia
February 29, 2012

1

Why Conflict Happens

Although it is utilized almost universally, a hierarchical structure is a peculiar model for churches to employ. Such a model gives one person authority over others for the purpose of determining what is organizationally expedient, and requires that the needs of people give way to organizational interests. Secular companies choose this model because advancement of the corporation is the top priority. It is understood that operational control must be placed in the hands of one person.... But it is a strange choice for churches, because churches should value the needs of people above those of the organization.

—John Setser, *Broken Hearts, Shattered Trust*

St. Elmo, AL—August 7, 2011

Mobile County local law enforcement had to be called in to investigate a fight that occurred between staff members after Sunday services at New Welcome Baptist Church.

The brawl broke out when Rev. Darryl Riley informed the church's music minister of six years, Simone Moore, that it was time to step down. Pastor Riley handed Moore his final paycheck—apparently in the presence of the church's deacons and Moore's own mother. Mr. Moore wasn't happy with the amount on the check and responded by pulling out a Taser®, which he (allegedly) used on the pastor. A melee ensued, and before it ended, Moore's mother had been stabbed in the hand by Harvie Hunt, a 59-year-old deacon, who was wielding "a long, 18-inch knife," according to this account.

> Six people ended up in the hospital after the fight. The deacon turned himself in and was charged with second-degree assault. Moore turned himself in a day later, and faces a third-degree assault charge. Whew.
>
> "Three obvious lessons are to be learned from this story," said the musician who shared this surreal tale on his blog:
>
> 1. Music ministers should not be allowed to carry Tasers®, stun guns, or other electroshock weaponry during church services.
> 2. A deacon should never stab the parents, male or female, of church staff members.
> 3. An "18-inch knife" is not a knife, but a sword. And deacons should not be bringing swords into church meetings. [1]

Whether they tase each other or not, most clergy and musicians do not deal well with conflict. In fact, one of the qualities we have in common is a fervent desire to avoid conflict. We not only avoid it, we deny it, hope it will go away, and minimize its impact. And none of this works, because when the conflict is not addressed, lives can be shattered and churches can be damaged.

Eric Routley, the esteemed English pastor, musician, and hymn writer, argued in his influential book *Church Music and Theology*, "So long as the theologian and the artist refuse to communicate with one another; as long as the theologian regards the artist as fundamentally a temperamental trifler, and the artist the theologian as an obstinate and ignorant theorist, the best we shall get is patronage from church to music, together with tentative moralisms from musicians to musicians. At worst it will be, as it often in practice is, a wicked waste of an opportunity for glorifying God through fruitful partnership."[2]

The inability to deal constructively with conflict is a prime example of such a wicked waste. Every conflict has at least two sides and two contributors. The problem is not always caused by only one party.

Musicians can be elitist, controlling, difficult, demanding, and uncompromising. Clergy also can be elitist, controlling, difficult, demanding, and uncompromising. Acknowledging that both clergy and musicians contribute to conflict in their working relationship, here are confessions from each.

Confessions of a Musician

We can be our own worst enemies, but we don't have to be!

Musicians work very hard studying music, learning the music of their instruments, choral music, and church music. We spend a lifetime in this pursuit, often beginning as young children, usually starting with the piano. We sing in church, school, and collegiate choirs, perhaps continuing into adulthood by singing in a community chorus. We grow in our taste and knowledge of different genres and styles of music, and we develop an appreciation for the ability of music to connect with the musicians with whom we work and with the listener.

In spite of many years of study and immersion in music, there is much that we do not know. One of the phrases I find myself using frequently is, "Well, they didn't teach me *that* in music school." This is not to denigrate the education I had, but to say that there is so much to learn, including non-musical skills that are essential to being an effective church musician. There are so many ways to grow and there are so many pitfalls of which we are not aware. Here are some of the traps into which we can fall that render us and our ministry less effective than might otherwise be.

Confession 1: Some of us find it difficult not to be in command at all times. We expect choirs to sing on our cue and cut off at our direction. We dictate the tone color we think is appropriate as well as many other aspects of the musical score; they are all interpreted through our lens. We need to recognize that there are differences between life in the rehearsal room or sanctuary and life outside these spaces, where we are not the ones in control.

Confession 2: We take matters into our own hands. Often musicians, knowing and caring about worship as we do, are put in charge of planning the liturgy. Sometimes this extends to stage directing, and the problem comes when this is done without sufficient knowledge or without sufficient tact. Sometimes our need to control elements of the service gets out of control itself. A student pastor recounts such precipitous actions of one musician.

> I had to assert my pastoral authority with the musician when the musician changed the music I had selected as the worship leader and I were walking down the aisle for Sunday worship. She walked over to the organist and told him not to play a hymn I had selected because it did not complement the one she selected for the anthem. She also told him to play a choral response to the Lord's Prayer that I had told her we would not do.

> This past Sunday she again tried to change the order of worship without consulting me. I explained to her that I spend a lot of prayerful time in planning worship. Although I am open to suggestions and input, I cannot have her making changes just minutes before the worship service without consulting me. I also told her that her input is important, and it would be helpful if she would be willing to discuss the music with me ahead of time.[3]

Confession 3: Our insistence on perfection, ingrained in us from our earliest lessons, may inhibit our trying new things. Our earliest piano lessons focused on putting the right finger on the right key for the right length of time, with the right touch and weight. Everything was about doing the right thing. Lessons on other instruments had parallel requirements. As trained musicians, we should by now recognize that there is, in reality, room for a great deal of nuance and interpretation in all things musical, but this is sometimes hard for musicians to accept. There can be a steep learning curve as the right way becomes the most effective way or simply a different way.

Confession 4: Linked to our desire for perfection is the fact that we do not always value people over performance. As church leaders, we really cannot allow our goals for the excellence of the performance, for the diction or the tone color or the accuracy of the notes, to obscure the fact that *we are in ministry,* and in ministry, people are more important than performance. The dedication of the members of the group, their sense of community, and their desire to minister through music are part of what they bring to worship. Thomas Are, in his book *Faithsong,* affirms, "A minister of music who believes that the function of musical performance outweighs the responsibility to minister to people will not succeed in what matters most."[4]

Confession 5: We get annoyed when things do not go according to plan. This desire for perfection can creep in at moments that seem more consequential at the time than they really are. For instance, when a musical selection in a worship service was skipped by the clergy, a musician in my acquaintance turned off the organ and left the service! There are instances when we are disturbed that the silence after a poignant piece is shattered by someone making an impromptu announcement about the car with its lights left on in the parking lot. When we have planned worship carefully, many of us become impatient when its effect seems to be negated, however unintentionally, by others.

Confession 6: We are used to planning and practicing ahead, and it is sometimes hard to work with people who operate in a different time frame and who have a different definition of what constitutes "ahead." This is actually one of the most frequent complaints of musicians. Perhaps we can do something about it, beginning with a conversation about why we need the information ahead of time. It might not occur to someone else that we not only need time to select the music that will best support the sermon and scripture, we also need time to order it if it is not in the library, and time for the choir to learn it once it arrives.

Confession 7: We are not doing ourselves any favors when we refuse to meet with the clergy or staff. "What? They're the ones who refuse to meet with *me*!" you might be thinking. That may be the case in some situations, but numerous clergy have complained that even when staff meetings have been planned around the schedule of the musician, the musician does not attend. The negative effect is compounded when the musician then does the "passive-aggressive thing" and complains about being excluded from worship planning discussions.

Confession 8: Lack of flexibility can be a stumbling block for us. There is an increasing need for musicians to be flexible—whether it is in terms of genre, style of music, or type of service. Our college instruction or the private lessons we took many years ago may not have given us the skills that are needed by congregations in the twenty-first century. Broadening our skills really is no longer an option, as churches are increasingly requiring diverse musical programs; musicians serving these churches will have to be able to meet those needs. Musicians not only need to have a wider range of skills, but also a wider choice of repertoire. Pledge never to say the words "over my dead body" when it comes to music in worship. Of course, it's not that anything goes, but if it is music we truly believe is inappropriate for worship, we should be willing to discuss it. We need to listen to the reasons that music has been suggested and need to be willing to articulate our reasons for believing that it is not appropriate.

A student pastor wrote me: "The musician has grown up in the church and despises any kind of change or new ideas in worship. She has said that the new hymnal supplement is going to be the downfall of worship."[5] What a regrettable situation, and at a time when resisting the need to expand our repertoire is viewed by some as threatening our very survival as church musicians. "In recent times," an organist writes, "many innovations are occurring in worship service music. Some of my colleagues have stayed in the same Baroque era in which they were educated, rejecting contemporary trends." She cites other organists who refuse "to participate in a contemporary service, or use a piano, or introduce to the choir 'new' music," concluding that she herself is "increasingly convinced that flexibility can only enhance our ministry as musicians today."[6]

Confession 9: Boundaries can be a challenge; it is easy and may seem natural to make the choirs your support groups. It takes constant vigilance on our part not to share information with choir members that should not be shared, whether it is inside information about the church or personal information concerning a member of the congregation.

Confession 10: We can be divas. A recent blog conversation among musicians discussed an organist who insisted on making hymn-playing a recital, often playing so loudly that the congregation could not hear itself sing or completely overpowering the ensemble that was being accompanied. I cringed reading these messages, as the numerous musicians being described clearly do not have a sense of their place in the full picture of music-making in worship. Here's one example:

> There's nothing worse than an organist who blasts or plays mini-recitals for hymns! The congregation that can't hear the melody, can't hear themselves, can't worship without frustration. This is just as bad as screeching guitars. We as musicians must remember that the time for corporate singing is just that, not a time for showing our talents to the exclusion of others. Anthems and special music are the times for those gifts. We need to remember that we are there to lead congregational song, regardless of style.[7]

Confession 11: In focusing our energies on the performing ensembles and our own practice, we sometimes lose perspective on the institution of which we are only one part. It is critical that we support the church's other programs, that we offer classes in the education area when asked, that we partner with the mission program in fundraising for special needs, that we see ourselves as a part of the whole body that is the church.

Music in the church is *ministry*. Musicians are *vehicles* through which the love of God and the message of salvation flow. We are not the end point, we are the conveyers of the Word through notes played and sung. While our ineptness should not be a distraction to the effective delivery of the Word, perfection is not our goal; having the message heard, felt, and taken away is.

Confessions of a Pastor

The Rev. Dr. Carol Cook Moore, a colleague from Wesley Theological Seminary with whom I work in worship planning, offers these confessions from her point of view as a clergywoman who served in congregational ministry for twenty-five years before joining the seminary faculty.

Confession 1: Of all the responsibilities we hold in parish ministry, the effectiveness of worship is held to be one of the most important for most clergy. Given that, we often feel the service rises and falls on our shoulders. We bring our theological ethos and are not prepared to share and teach the underpinnings of that ethos. We function out of a set of assumptions that are often not transparent.

Some are practical and some are theological. Whatever the case, we easily forget that not everyone is on the same page, and in terms of worship preparation, planning, and leading, being on the same page is essential! This can also lead us to being unable to ask for help because we believe, or think others believe, that we should have all the answers. This behavior can fuel miscommunication and power struggles leading to a lack of teamwork. It is important to admit what we do not know and to seek out constructive answers and solutions. Clergy and musicians can be a tremendous resource for one another. That requires admitting that we need and want such a resource!

Confession 2: We, too, are human. We want to be accepted, liked, and valued for our work. We easily fall into the trap of becoming co-dependent and therefore making decisions out of this need, rather than a healthier approach to working together with our musician colleagues. Rather than coming to the musician with our complaints, concerns, or suggestions, we clergy can make inappropriate, disrespectful comments to others regarding their work or the choir's ability. If we are not proactive in forming healthy patterns of communication and accountability, we can participate in a congregant's attempt to isolate one of us or triangulate us in patterns that only breed contempt and break down any hope of a partnership.

Confession 3: Many of us are given the authority to oversee worship. Some denominations say in their polity that the senior minister is in charge of/responsible for worship. This easily becomes a platform for control. Some of us want to control every aspect of worship either because we believe we are best suited, because we have to make sure it is good since the buck stops here, or because we do not know how to share ministry and still be the one who is ultimately in charge.

Confession 4: We know deep down that we are *not* in control! If we believe in the power of the Holy Spirit flowing through the worship experience, then we know that, ultimately, this is about God at work and not our proficiency or success. We also can speak volumes on the actions of children, ushers, musicians, and lectors whose involvement in worship is out of our control! However, we can respond to this knowledge and these experiences by seeking more control rather than empowering trained and effective leadership.

Confession 5: We can become envious of the power and effectiveness of our musician colleagues, as well as their incredible gifts. You, the musician can create a crescendo that stirs the hearts of the parishioners more deeply than any sermon of ours. If a choir is to have any effectiveness, it requires your leadership and their loyalty as well as ability to work their voices together. How wonderful it would be if the entire ministry of the church could function as smoothly as a four-part anthem. You also have to create community in order to foster the ministry of the choir. You are a group. If we feel isolated in our ministry, we can become very envious of your relationship with the choir.

Confession 6: We can easily focus on the sermon as if it were the only important act of worship. For some congregations, preaching is the focal point or climax of the service. However, that does not mean that the other parts of worship are not equally important and do not deserve equal attention in planning and synchronizing with one another.

Confession 7: For some of us, it is very difficult to admit we are wrong. There is something about the power we are given and the way we respond to expectations from congregations and our superiors that seems to lead us toward defensiveness instead of self-evaluation and seeking opportunities for growth personally and professionally. In order for our leadership to be trusted, we need to be able to make sincere apologies and to move toward reconciliation and change when and where it is needed. When we come to a point of disagreement, we need to be able to foster resolution.

Like all human relationships, the relationship between the musician and the clergy takes work. This work involves listening, respecting, speaking honestly, building trust, and learning *how* to be partners in ministry. We are partners with distinct gifts, responsibilities, and authority—yet, partners. How else can we live out Paul's image of the church as the body of Christ?

Conflict within the Church

With the potential for seemingly inevitable conflict between clergy and musician, how are we to view this situation? Are we looking for ways to avoid all conflict (as if that were truly possible!)? No. The truth is that conflict can be productive. A broader perspective allows for decisions in the best interest of an institution and its mission over individual preferences, and people who are passionate about their ministry may well not agree about what is important and the best way to achieve it. This healthy disagreement can actually result in productive discussion and a better decision at the end. The results can be positive, as long as the arguments do not get personal and remain issue-oriented.

What is it about churches that can cause conflict to become unproductive, or worse? One reason may be the desire for control on the part of church members and lack of consequences for their actions. Donors often feel their support should buy influence. When there is conflict between staff and clergy, church members and boards (vestries, trustees, or deacons) largely side with the clergy. They defend the clergy and ignore the conflict, even when church policies have been violated, sometimes even in the face of clear workplace abuse. Why? It's the fear factor. Congregations worry that the church will fall apart if they call the clergy to account. They feel that they are better off with pastors whose flaws are known than with whatever person the "clergy lottery" might bring them as a replacement; or they recognize the difficulties a long interim period between clergy can cause a congregation; or they simply minimize the situation and stay with the status quo. Denominational judicatories may be unwilling to listen carefully or compassionately to the complaints of staff members and they may not pay attention to members of the congregation who express concern that there really is something wrong in a situation.

In churches with a strong committee infrastructure, musicians feel protected because there is a process in place through which their concerns can be addressed. A manipulative senior pastor, however, can stack committees with personal supporters; after the customary three–year rotation of committee membership, everyone on the committee will have been appointed with the senior pastor's blessing (and may well be in the senior pastor's pocket). If this sounds paranoid, I'm sorry; it happens, over and over.

Church governance can be a closed network that leaves the musician on the outside, with no voice and no recourse, and therefore no choice but to leave. This often causes grief, not only for the musician, the musician's family and friends, choir members, and the congregation—it can also split the church. A substantial number of churches have taken years to recover—some have not yet recovered—after the departure of a beloved musician who was forced out by the clergy.

Specific strategies for healthy ways of dealing with conflict are discussed in Chapter 7.

Notes

1. "How Not to Handle Conflict Between Church Staff Members," posted on August 24, 2011 by Jason Boyett. (http://www.faithvillage.com/2011/08/how-not-to-handle-conflict-between-church-staff-members).

2. Eric Routley, *Church Music and Theology*, quoted in Paul Westermeyer, *The Church Musician*, Minneapolis: Augsburg Fortress, 1997, 87.

3. Sherri Cormer-Cox, "Interview with a Church Musician" written for Wesley Chapel Choir, Wesley Theological Seminary, Washington, D.C., December, 2011.

4. Thomas L. Are, *Faithsong: A New Look at the Ministry of Music,* Philadelphia: The Westminster Press, 1981, 50.

5. Comer-Cox, "Interview."

6. [Name withheld], e-mail, September 21, 2010.

7. Shelley Reel, e-mail to author, February 22, 2012.

2

Shared Visions: The Importance of Clergy-Musician Teams

Now there are varieties of gifts, but the same Spirit; and there are varieties of skills, but the same Lord; and there are varieties of talents, but it is the same God who activates all of them in everyone. To each is given the manifestation of the Spirit for the common good. To one is given through the Spirit the utterance of preaching, and to another the utterance of song according to the same Spirit, to another administration by the same Spirit, to another gifts of conducting by the one Spirit, to another the leadership of worship, to another skill at the organ or piano, to another the discernment of ways to lead the congregation in its mission, to another techniques for effective rehearsals, to both the interpretation of the Word of God in song and speech. All these are activated by one and the same Spirit, who allots to each one individually just as the Spirit chooses.

—1 Corinthians 12:4-11 (paraphrased)

The focus of this book is on creating a situation in which we can best use the talents and gifts God has given us. Discerning how to do this is one of the greatest challenges and opportunities of our ministries. All of our skills are needed for effective worship planning and enabling church programs, and our work will be most productive when it is done as a team. As Henry Ford said, "Coming together is a beginning. Keeping together is progress. Working together is success."[1]

We recognize the existence of many kinds of teams—sales teams, research teams, sports teams—and the many definitions of team. Some are informal: "A team is a group of people who go out of their way to make each other look good."[2] Others are more specific: "A team has two or more people; it has a specific performance objective or recognizable goal to be attained; and coordination of activity among the members of the team is required for the attainment of the team goal or objective."[3] Or this, from the Harvard Business School: "A team is a small number of people with complementary skills who are committed to a common purpose, performance goals, and approach for which they hold themselves mutually accountable."[4]

The number of books, articles, and blogs on the subject of teams, teamwork, or team building is vast and growing daily. Because it is a concern so prevalent today, we can easily think we know all about teams. Sports teams probably get the most press. People stay up late watching a favorite football or baseball team on TV. My husband and I are big college basketball fans. When the NCAA basketball tournament known as "March Madness" begins, we are hooked. We love cheering for our alma mater and are intrigued as we watch the players develop year after year in skill and in their sense of place on the team.

Red Auerbach, longtime professional basketball coach, famously said, "One person seeking glory doesn't accomplish much; everything we've done has been the result of people working together to meet our common goals."[5] More recently, Mike Krzyzewski, Duke University's basketball coach for over three decades, described his recruiting philosophy. He looks not only for talent, but for players who are good communicators and who have the potential for being leaders. "Leadership is plural, not singular." He goes on to say, "As you become more secure as a leader, it gets easier to share leadership, to empower others."[6]

...talent wins games, but teamwork and intelligence win championships.

John Maxwell, in *Teamwork 101,* recounts a story about a winning team that never had a single player who led the league in scoring. It had many excellent players, but they were not out to show off their individual talent or rack up impressive personal statistics. They were there to do what they could to enable the team to do its best. With this perspective, it becomes clear, as Michael Jordan says, that "talent wins games, but teamwork and intelligence win championships."[7] Maxwell continues:

> The old rules of traditional, hierarchical, high-external-control, top-down management are being dismantled: they simply aren't working any longer. They are being replaced by a new form of "control"... that enables [people] to be driven by motivation *inside* them toward achiev-

> ing a common purpose. This has changed the role of manager from one who drives results and motivation from the outside in, to one who is a servant-leader—one who seeks to draw out, inspire, and develop the best and the highest within people from the inside out.[8]

There is a powerful teamwork component to the terms used by the late theologian from Yale Divinity School, Letty Russell, as she distinguishes between the " 'power of purpose' in contrast to the 'power of position.' "[9] Lovett Weems, director of the G. Douglass Lewis Center for Church Leadership at Wesley Theological Seminary, echoes her thinking:

> It is the church's mission and the vision for a particular congregation that must guide all ministries among the ordained, other staff, and laity. Christian authority is always about the fulfillment of God's vision. When leaders take their eyes off the larger vision, and focus instead on where they stand in relationship to others in a hierarchy, then energy is misdirected and leadership ceases to be faithful.[10]

He has a lot of company. "Beginning now and extending into the foreseeable future," says Larry Dill of The Institute for Clergy Excellence, "effective worship must be created in teams."[11] How does this take place? This happens by creating a shared vision, which "inspires each person to stretch and reach deeper within himself or herself, and to use everyone's unique talents in whatever way is necessary to independently and interdependently achieve that shared vision."[12]

Teamwork

It is practically impossible to pick up a magazine or read a newspaper without seeing an article on teamwork. Teamwork is widely regarded as *the best, if not the only way,* to build success. Management consultants say this; public relations people say this; behavioral scientists say this; and any of us who work with people simply know it to be true. People are much more interested in a goal when they have had some say in both defining what the goal is and in deciding how it will be achieved. In church work there is a single overarching goal—effective ministry—which is achieved by different means according to the organization's needs and the available talent. The bottom line is measured, not in corporate profits, but in the ability of the church to serve God and minister to its members.

Relationships in which each has the other's best interests at heart include a variety of elements: caring for each other, acknowledging mutual dependence, and acknowledging similarities and differences, strengths and weaknesses. In a healthy relationship, social needs are met and common goals affirmed. It is a collegial, not a hierarchical model.

Webster's New Collegiate Dictionary gives as a first definition for the word, collegial: "Marked by power or authority vested equally in each of a number of colleagues." However, applying this definition to clergy-musician teams is anything but easy.

In terms of the polity set forth by many denominations, clergy have final authority in all matters relating to the church. I do not know a single musician who does not acknowledge this. While giving clergy final authority, it is equally clear that many denominations' governance policies explicitly call for clergy and musicians to work together. For instance, the *Constitution and Canons of The Episcopal Church* (2006) state:

> [T]he Member of the Clergy shall have final authority in the administration of matters pertaining to music. In fulfilling this responsibility the Member of the Clergy shall seek assistance from persons skilled in music. *Together* [emphasis added] they shall see that music is appropriate to the context in which is it used.[13]

The Presbyterian Church (USA) *Book of Order* states:

> Where there is a choir director or other musical leader, the pastor and that person will confer to ensure that anthems and other musical offerings are appropriate for the particular service. The session should see that these conferences take place appropriately and on a regular basis.[14]

Music comprises a significant portion of the services in most churches, and a productive relationship between the clergy and those who direct the music is essential. One pastor writes:

> There is never the sense that "This is something you are doing for me." There is always the sense that this is something we are doing together and with the congregation. That creates a sense of partnership—between the rector and the musician, between the principal musician and the other musicians, and between the principal musician and the congregation. Partnership, partnership, partnership.[15]

The cost of poor clergy-musician relations is high. Without a solid partnership, relationships throughout the church may be affected, even destroyed. A parish may be divided into camps, one backing the clergy and another backing the musician. Lives may be damaged, members may leave the church, and such rifts have the potential to create problems that are often beyond repair.

Qualities Clergy and Musicians Share as a Basis for Team Building

- *Highly intuitive.* Worship leaders spend their careers developing a finely-honed intuition that allows them to have a keen feel for the pace of the service and its "EKG," its moments of tension and relaxation, excitement and contemplation. "Both clergy and musicians deal with the world and make decisions more often using information best described as subjective," says Rev. David Moores, "not hard facts or objective data. This use of the subjective opens both types to much greater creativity and imagination, but it also causes them to act much more decisively on the basis of their feelings alone."[16]

- *Highly motivated.* The description of workaholic is often not far from the truth. Both are prone to working long hours and juggling many demands. Both are prone to getting stressed out, especially when the church calendar is crowded, but also when less is going on in the life of the church, even though their pace may not slacken.

- *A sense of call.* While clergy are generally accepted as having been called to their work, musicians aren't always seen quite the same way in terms of a vocational call.

William Sloane Coffin, the late Yale University chaplain and pastor of Riverside Church in New York City, went to great lengths to distinguish between "career" and "calling" in his book *A Passion for the Possible.* He cited the writing of Professor William May of Southern Methodist University, who observed that both the word "car" and the word "career" come from the Latin word *carerra*, for "racetrack," suggesting

> that a car and a career both have you going in circles rapidly and competitively.... A car is an auto-mobile, a self-driven vehicle. It frees you from traveling with others. To Professor May it represents "glass-enwrapped privacy as you speed down public thoroughfares toward your own private destination."
>
> "Calling," on the other hand, comes from the Latin *vocatio* (vocation), from *vocare* (to call), which was defined by a seventeenth-century Puritan [clergyman] as "that whereunto God hath appointed us to serve the common good."[17]

Career-oriented people, Coffin notes, read books such as *Winning through Intimidation* and *Looking Out for Number One.* "A calling, by contrast, seeks the common good, not private gain. It sees service as the purpose of life, not something you might consider doing in your spare time. It is not against ambition, but considers ambition a good servant and a bad master."[18]

Clergy are usually considered to have been "called." Much of the new student orientation at the seminary where I teach is devoted to sharing ways the students have felt called and the meaning of that call. What is often not recognized is that this feeling of being called is very often also true of musicians. Many of us feel that we are called to be musicians serving in the church and that we are serving a particular church because of our abilities to meet the needs of those particular parishioners. One pastor writes:

> I value musicians who see what they do as calling and ministry, and not just performance or job ... who want to learn more about the parts of worship they don't know much about, and who are willing to risk to teach me what they know better, or to venture into the middle ground of true collaboration; who are spiritually mature and emotionally grounded. The best youth choir director in my daughter's high school singing days ensured that the choir was as effective a youth ministry as the mega-youth group, though on a smaller scale.[19]

Yes, musicians may just be looking for a job or may take a church position in order to have a fine organ on which to practice or perform, but very often the musician feels genuinely called to this work. "But it's my life," one abruptly-terminated musician cried. For many musicians, it *is* just that.

- *Nurturing.* Clergy nurture a congregation just as musicians nurture singers and instrumentalists. The pastoral aspects of a church musician's job are often the most critical. The success of a music program may well depend more on the ability to nurture than on one's choral techniques or fiery improvisations.

- *Conflict-avoiding and people-pleasing.* Even though we are in the people business, we cannot let pleasing others be the overriding goal of our lives. I heard one clergyman literally give two different answers to the same question—one at one end of the hallway, another at the opposite end. Being a people-pleaser, he told them exactly what they wanted to hear, regardless of what the truth actually was. Neither clergy nor musicians can afford to have this crippling need to be loved by everyone.

- *Under-compensated.* For their level of education and training, clergy and musicians often are underpaid in comparison to the salaries of many other professionals. This can be a significant stress factor. The senior pastor in point of fact *is* often the CEO of the congregation. Salaries are often totally out of proportion for the level of education, responsibility, and commitment, which may include administering a large budget and a complex organization, to say nothing of being on call for pastoral emergencies, being looked up to as the infallible spiritual leader of the congregation, having to attend multitudes of meetings, and meeting with multitudes of expectations.

Musicians, too, often work under stress, as they organize many people and run complex programs. If the musician is not employed full time by the church, s/he often works not one job, but two, or even three. This is not an easy way to earn a living. Guidelines issued by the American Guild of Organists and many denominations encourage institutions to compensate musicians fairly. But the challenges remain great, especially in difficult economic times.

- *Publicly evaluated weekly.* A clergyman I know tells a story, likely apocryphal, about another clergyman who customarily greeted his parishioners at the end of the service.

> Sam came through the line, and as he shook the pastor's hand, he said, "Pastor, your sermon reminded me of the peace and the mercy of God." The pastor was at first pretty pleased, even a little proud of himself, but then he decided to ask Sam exactly what he'd meant by his comment. "Well, Pastor," Sam said, "it reminded me of the peace of God because it passed all understanding. And it reminded me of the mercy of God in that I thought it would endure forever."

The clergyman telling the story is a great preacher and often receives compliments on his sermons, but instead of taking them at face value, he interprets them as having the subtext: "You were good today, but can you be as good again next week?"

Never underestimate the pressure of this evaluation factor. Unlike bureaucrats who may work on a project for years without seeing it completed, or someone whose work is not evaluated regularly, clergy and musician are constantly evaluated. The clergy's leadership of the service, the prayers, and the sermon; the musician's playing of the liturgy, anthems, responses, hymns and voluntaries—all are on view at every service, every week.

Fundamental Ways Clergy and Musicians Differ

- The pressures are different. Clergy are the chief executive officers of the church, having overall administrative oversight as well as responsibility for worship, spiritual leadership, and pastoral care. Musicians may also have administrative duties and may offer pastoral care, but their primary responsibility is for the music of worship and the musicians who give leadership in the services.

- Clergy and musicians may come to the table with differing attitudes about the way they should work together. Is the relationship supervisory or collegial?

- Clergy and musicians often have different educational backgrounds and different areas of expertise. William Bradley Roberts is entirely correct when he suggests the church might look radically different today if clergy and musicians received their training in the same environment.

> Most denominations are intentional and energetic in training their clergy. They expect that if clergy are to receive the tradition of the church and spend a lifetime leading parishes, they need to be properly prepared. Denominations set aside financial resources, bring together the best minds, build and equip campuses, and provide oversight by boards of interested leaders. That we don't give the same attention to the training of church musicians is outright negligence.[20]

- Clergy may assume musicians care only about the music, which is often totally wrong. While there may be musicians whose choice of music is based solely on the notes, many musicians care greatly about the text and work hard to ensure that the musical selections connect with the sermon and support the liturgy.

Differences, of course, have the potential of leading to conflict. Following are two scenarios for conflict described by M. Lee Orr in his book *The Church Music Handbook for Pastors and Musicians:*

> The autocrat in the pulpit acquired much of his or her imperialistic attitude in the seminary, where he or she learned to view a pastor as a divinely inspired Chief Executive Officer. In this wise and benevolent role the pastor shapes worship according to weekly insights, then bestows this prophetic vision upon the musician to fill out with musical connective tissue. And should the musician, working in the liturgical dark, select the wrong filler material, that only confirms the pastor's suspicions concerning the musician's liturgical ineptness. Or at the least, it betrays the musician's inexcusable inability to read the pastor's mind.[21]

Or its corollary:

> [The musician] acquired her autocracy in school. Pushed to sing and play as well as she possibly could, [she] developed a passion for excellence; and not just in performance but also in her musical selections. Her teachers constantly insisted that she study, listen to, and perform only the finest art music. When she continued on to complete her master's degree, she further refined her skills as well as her elitist attitude about what was best for worship.
>
> Later, when she took the education courses to become a teacher, she subtly internalized the profile—often a necessary teaching tool—of ex-

> plaining to people how to do things because she knew better. Sometimes this included explaining to [the pastor].[22]

Taken together, these scenarios would seem to be a pretty nice recipe for conflict. I know only one church where the pastor resigned because of the autocracy of the musician, but I can count many situations where the musician has resigned because of the autocracy of the clergy. This simply does not have to be the case. Orr offers one solution, albeit one much easier to say than to do.

The Power of Partnership

> Pastor and musician must abdicate their thrones, open themselves up to dialogue, and "move from pride to partnership".... Only in this way will worship regain its spiritual vigor, the congregation become empowered, and the church rise anew to face its challenge. Together, the minister and musician must each leave their fiefdoms of pulpit and choir loft and forge a partnership. For the pastor, this means stepping down from the lofty realms of being the CEO and standing on common ground with the musician, the rest of the staff, and the congregation. It also means that the musician must leave the secure artistic shelter behind the altar rail [or in the balcony] and join the entire church community—clergy and congregation—in worshiping together. Then everyone can join together as equal partners in making the liturgy as meaningful and dynamic as possible.[23]

With all that musicians and clergy have in common, why is it that differences in roles so often obscure the commonalities and lead to conflict? What steps need to be taken so that clergy and musicians begin to operate as a team instead of separate entities? To answer, here are a few suggestions for forming healthy and supportive relationships.

There is incalculable value in teams. Mountain-climbing expeditions succeed only with the support of a vast and committed array of team members. Major scientific discoveries are made and Nobel prizes are won by teams. Industries develop new products as individuals collaborate as a team. "... as the challenge escalates, the need for teamwork elevates."[24] That's the Law of Mount Everest—and, may I say, it should be the law of the church, too.

The importance of working together is not new. "There are many objects of great value," said statesman Daniel Webster, "which cannot be attained by unconnected individuals, but must be attained if at all, by association."[25] Also on point are the words of industrialist and philanthropist Andrew Carnegie, who observed, "It marks a big step in your development when you come to realize that other people can help you do a better job than you could do alone."[26]

More recently, the pastor-author-educator Charles Swindoll has written in *The Finishing Touch:*

> Nobody is a whole team.... We need each other. You need someone and someone needs you. Isolated islands we're not. To make this thing called life work, we gotta lean and support. And relate and respond. And give and take. And confess and forgive. And reach out and embrace and rely ... since none of us is a whole, independent, self-sufficient, super-capable, all-powerful hotshot, let's quit acting like we are. Life's lonely enough without our playing that silly role. The game is over. Let's link up.[27]

All of us is smarter than any of us is.

The results are better when we have had the input of many. This is the premise of the book, *The Wisdom of Crowds*. It is also one of the smartest strategies ever articulated. I heard it repeated often by J. Philip Wogaman, a truly collegial pastor with whom I worked for ten years: "All of us is smarter than any of us is." With a team there are many more perspectives on the table, higher-energy discussions, and a much wider span of ideas than any single individual could offer. Whether brainstorming for a worship service or a service project, a church staff will be more energized and create more and better ideas together than any of them could have created alone. A musician writes:

> My current relationship with my pastors is the best yet. Not only are they competent and creative, they know a lot about music, care a lot about music, and realize the power of music in worship. They invite me to be a part of team planning each week and it is wonderful collaborative effort. It's a church musician's dream come true. Looking back over my career, I had what I called "seven years of feast" followed by "four years of famine." The years of feast were led by a wise, brave senior pastor who encouraged us to take risks and think big. He empowered us professionally and personally and always had our back. During those years, the church really moved forward. When he retired, the church was assigned a dysfunctional pastor who, for various complicated reasons, was a disaster. The institutional ship really rocked and many jumped ship. That pastor knew nothing about music, cared nothing about music, and was basically clueless and incompetent. There was no communication or planning.[28]

Teamwork is not innate and, in many cases, working as a team can actually be a challenge. "We need to know how to set aside individual agendas so that a common understanding of a problem has an opportunity to develop," write

Carl Larson and Frank LaFasto. "We need to know how the activities of people can be coordinated and their efforts brought together within a structure that integrates and focuses, rather than diffuses. We need to know how to foster the trust and the sharing of information that will lead to the best decisions."[29]

Although it might not initially seem so, working as a team can be more efficient in the long run. Work is certainly more fun when shared. This is true for musicians, who spend so much time in solitary activities such as practicing; it is also true for clergy, who must spend significant time alone in sermon preparation.

Of course, it is easier for the pastor to choose the hymns and toss the list into the musician's mail box in the church office than it is to discuss thoughtfully and prayerfully the service, the scripture readings, the special themes, the elements of the service that occur every week and the elements that are unique to that particular service. It is also easier for the musician to choose the anthem (and perhaps the hymns) than to discuss thoughtfully and prayerfully these choices and other options with the clergy or other members of the staff.

I have spent a lot of years planning worship—it is one of my favorite things in the world to do—and while I bring ideas to these meetings that are pretty creative, there has rarely been an instance when someone on the team did not come up with an idea that improved on mine. Additionally, in articulating the reasons for my choice of a hymn or an anthem, I often find my mind ping-ponging around options that might work even better.

While forming a team may not be easy or intuitive, teamwork has the potential to be enormously rewarding. It is also my conviction that this teamwork is essential to effective parish ministry.

Notes

1. "Think Exist Quotations," http://thinkexist.com/quotes/henry_ford, accessed February 25, 2012.

2. http://www.articlesbase.com/non-fiction-articles/the-value-of-teamwork-114764.html, accessed February 25, 2012.

3. Carl E. Larson and Frank M.J. LaFasto, *Teamwork: What Must Go Right/ What Can Go Wrong,* Newbury Park, CA: SAGE Publications, 1989, 19.

4. Jon R. Katzenbach and Douglas K. Smith, "The Discipline of Teams," *Harvard Business Review* 83, no. 7/8 (July–August 2005): 163.

5. John C. Maxwell, *Teamwork 101: What Every Leader Needs to Know,* Nashville: Thomas Nelson, 2008, 20.

6. Sim B. Sitkin and J. Richard Hackman, "Developing Team Leadership: An Interview with Coach Mike Krzyzewski," *Academy of Management Learning and Education* 10, no. 3 (2011): 494–501.

7. Maxwell, *Teamwork 101*, 22.

8. Robert K. Greenleaf, *Servant Leadership: A Journey into the Nature of Legitimate Power & Greatness,* New York: Paulist Press, 1977, 3.

9. Kevin E. Lawson, *How to Thrive in Associate Staff Ministry,* Bethesda, MD: Alban Institute, 2000, vi.

10. *Ibid.*

11. Hugh Ballou, *Moving Spirits, Building Lives: The Church Musician As Transformational Leader,* Blacksburg: SynerVision International, Inc., 2005, v.

12. Greenleaf, 3.

13. The Episcopal Church, Regarding Music and Ministry (Canon II 6.1–4), *Constitution and Canons of The Episcopal Church,* New York: Church Publishing Incorporated, 2006.

14. Presbyterian Church (USA), Pastor and Choir Director [W-1.4005b], *The Constitution of the Presbyterian Church* (USA), Part II: *Book of Order,* 2009–2011, Louisville, KY: The Office of the General Assembly, 2009.

15. *Ibid.,* 99.

16. David R. Moores, "Clergy-Organist Relationships," *The American Organist* 19, no. 8, (August, 1985): 46–47.

17. William Sloane Coffin, *A Passion for the Possible*, 2nd ed. Louisville: Westminster/John Knox Press, 2004, 77.

18. *Ibid.,* 77–78.

19. Cynthia Horn Burkert, e-mail to author, October, 2011.

20. William Bradley Roberts, *Music and Vital Congregations: A Practical Guide for Clergy,* New York: Church Publishing Incorporated, 2009, 36.

21. N. Lee Orr, *The Church Music Handbook for Pastors and Musicians,* Nashville: Abingdon Press, 1991, 43–44.

22. *Ibid.,* 45–46.

23. *Ibid.,* 47.

24. Maxwell, *Teamwork 101*, 32.

25. Larson and LaFasto, 13.

26. Maxwell, *Teamwork 101,* 9.

27. Swindoll, *The Finishing Touch,* quoted in Maxwell, *Teamwork 101,* 12.

28. Janna Kisner, e-mail to author, October 12, 2011.

29. Lawson and LaFasto, 14–15.

3
The Servant-Leader

It is true that the church is like no other institution. It has its origin in an ancient project of God to raise up a people who will be a blessing to the nations. It is uniquely anchored in the ministry of Jesus and his disciples. It is redeemed by Jesus' death on the cross and saved from historical oblivion by his resurrection. It is ignited by the Spirit's visit at Pentecost to animate and equip persons to share good news to the ends of the earth. By God's provident interventions it journeys onward through the ages as sign and witness to God's final reign.

But the church is still an institution. It acts and feels and behaves like an institution. It has a life apart from the contributions and detractions of its individual members. It has collective memory and an evolving collective narrative. Like a family system it is a force field of scripts, codes, synergistic love, and scapegoating. Like a corporate culture it has rites of initiations, undeniable artifacts, and chains of accountability and attention. And, like virtually every human institution known to us...it recognizes its leaders, identifies with them emotionally, and incessantly points to them in deference, praise, or blame.... The church's hunger for a language of church leadership is ancient, recurring, and certain.

—Lewis A. Parks and Bruce C. Birch
Ducking Spears, Dancing Madly

Leadership in the church—the people who are called to be leaders, and the ways they exercise it—has been the subject of many books. We want desperately to get it right in an age where means are confused with ends, and there is little agreement on what "right" really is. In this chapter, we identify the most important qualities of effective leaders, regardless of their particular role in church leadership. These qualities have a direct role in enabling a productive and mutually fulfilling relationship between clergy and musicians.

Looking within

Servant-Leaders

In Robert Greenleaf's influential book *Servant Leadership,* Peter Senge writes in the Afterword that "The servant-leader is servant first ... as opposed to wanting power, influence, fame or wealth."[1] A servant-leader asks: Do my own needs take second place to the needs of others? "Do those served grow as persons? Do they, *while being served,* become healthier, wiser, freer, more autonomous, more likely themselves to become servants?"[2] When one chooses to be a servant-leader, influence, power, position, and a desire to control are less important than serving others. Stephen Covey, the best-selling author of *The Seven Habits of Highly Effective People,* observes, "It has generally been my experience that the very top people of truly great organizations are servant-leaders. They are the most humble, the most reverent, the most open, the most teachable, the most respectful, the most caring, and the most determined."[3]

Yet, clergy and musicians are all used to being in charge. As choral conductors and worship leaders, we are in key positions to determine the elements of worship as well as its pace and quality. While in one sense we are in charge, we are ultimately servants of God and servants of the liturgy. It is not about us, our interpretation, or our amazing skills. Our role is one of enabling the prayer and praise of the gathered community.

"The clergy and musicians who experience the smoothest and most productive working relationships," Charlotte Kroeker writes in *The Sounds of Our Offerings,* "embrace servant leadership styles in which their common tasks and respect for each other are the dominant factors."[4] This is far from the "my way or the highway" motto that characterizes some leaders. When servant leadership is activated, the potential is huge, and, as William Bradley Roberts states in *Music and Vital Congregations,* "the power of God's Spirit is truly unleashed."[5]

Humility

Effective leaders bring out the leadership in others.

This quality, generally considered non-negotiable, counts as a subset of servant-leadership. Many brilliant individuals and powerful preachers have also been persons of deep humility and self-effacement. "The most effective leaders," report Carl E. Larson and Frank M. J. LaFasto in *Teamwork, What Must Go Right/What Can Go Wrong,* "were those who subjugated their ego needs in favor of the team's goal. They allowed team members to take an active part in shaping the destiny of the team's effort. They allowed them to decide, to make choices, to act, to do something meaningful. The result of this approach was the creation of the 'multiplier effect.' It created a contagion among team members to unlock their own leadership abilities.... Effective leaders bring out the leadership in others."[6]

Pastoral Flexibility

The effective leader is not always the leader. That individual fills different roles at different times, knows which role is most appropriate in a given circumstance, and is able to switch roles between leader, peer, coach, and follower without skipping a beat. Effective leaders also are unconcerned about who gets credit for any success because their dedication is to the team, not to themselves.

Effective pastoral and musical leaders balance and shift roles on several planes. Pastoral concerns must always inform the way we approach our roles. There is a fine line between a desire for excellence in performance and working at it so relentlessly that we damage relationships in the process. For example, pastors must not allow rigid adherence to a deadline to override personal concern for a staff member when the delay was caused by a family emergency. Musicians cannot become so focused on the technical or musical aspects of a piece that we embarrass singers or call people out on their mistakes—behavior that totally misses the point of the music and its ministry. According to Kroeker, strong pastors believe that "the most effective church musicians combine strong pastoral ministry with the abilities of good technical musicians."[7]

Self-Knowledge

Leaders need to have a realistic sense of personal strengths and weaknesses. This knowledge allows us to seek out people who have needed skills we ourselves lack. For example, I am truly challenged when it comes to space perception. So when I need to place musicians in a particular configuration, I seek the help of others who do that much better than I could.

It is also helpful to know our own limits: how many late-night meetings or rehearsals can we manage in a given week? How many extra classes, speaking engagements, or recitals? Knowing when enough is bordering on too much is crucial for our health and sanity as well as important to our families and friends.

Self-Confidence

Self-confidence must not be confused with egotism. Being self-confident means having a sure sense of one's skills and value as a human being and a child of God. Many times when leaders adopt bravado, it is really a mask designed to cover up their insecurities. They fear showing human weakness and revealing that they really do not know everything. As Henri Nouwen wrote in *Out of Solitude,* "We are afraid of being judged and found wanting.... You are fine as who you are. Have faith in yourself, instead of requiring approval from others, and then get on with being connected in community."[8]

Genuine, healthy self-confidence is the mark of knowing we are valued for who we are and not for what we do. One of the greatest lessons Nouwen teaches is that our value as human beings does not rest on our accomplishments, the number of people in our choirs, the size of our budgets or congregations. Those are totally irrelevant factors that, in fact, can actually inhibit our ministry. Nouwen writes:

> When we start being too impressed by the results of our work, we slowly come to the erroneous conviction that life is one large scoreboard where someone is listing the points to measure our worth. And before we are fully aware of it, we have sold our soul to the many grade-givers.... Then we become what the world makes us. We are intelligent because someone gives us a high grade. We are helpful because someone says thanks.... And we are important because someone considers us indispensable.... And the more we allow our accomplishments—the results of our actions—to become the criteria of our self-esteem, the more we are going to walk on our mental and spiritual toes, never sure if we will be able to live up to the expectations which we created by our last successes. In many people's lives, there is a nearly diabolic chain in which their anxieties grow according to their successes.[9]

Self-Discipline

No matter how smart or talented we are, we must be disciplined and organized. James C. Collins, in his book *Good to Great,* talks about the wider value of a culture of discipline: "When you have disciplined people, you don't need hierarchy. When you have disciplined thought, you don't need bureaucracy. When you have disciplined action, you don't need excessive controls."[10]

Discipline is thoroughly ingrained in most musicians. As youth we practiced while the other children were outside playing after school; in college we gave up Friday night parties to prepare for a recital the next day. Similarly, clergy demonstrate discipline in the way they prepare their sermons and plan worship well in advance, which helps not only the musician but enhances the work of others giving leadership to the service.

Tasks need to be prioritized so that colleagues can plan ahead for the long term as well as for the more immediate future. There's the "80/20 rule," which says that we will be most effective when we spend eighty percent of our time and effort on the twenty percent of the responsibilities that will truly make a difference: sermon preparation, pastoral care, worship planning (for clergy); music selection, worship planning, practice (for musicians); for both: meetings, e-mails and calls to members of the choirs and congregation, allowing time for the occasional unplanned drop in.

Personal Integrity

Effective leaders not only communicate honestly, we truly are people of integrity. Our words and actions are consistent; we demonstrate in our lives what we say we believe. People are confident that we will speak the truth, even if it casts us in an unfavorable light. We recognize and respect boundaries, make sure not to do anything that leaves our integrity open to question, and follow through on commitments.

Part of being a person of integrity is keeping confidences. If someone shares personal information, one must request their permission before passing it on to others or voicing it in public prayer; without that permission, the confidence has been violated. Similarly, gossip is on the "don't go there" list. Yes, it can be amusing, or even entertaining, to share information about others—especially in a way that allows us to feel just a bit superior to be in the know. But it has the potential of being terribly damaging to the person about whom one is speaking, and it damages the one doing the gossiping. The urge to gossip can never be indulged if a leader hopes to maintain the people's trust.

Creativity

Whether brainstorming with a worship planning team or engaging in meditation or yoga alone, we are open to our God-given creative inspiration. Creativity can involve doing something for the first time or doing familiar things in new ways. The possibilities are countless: a new approach to a sermon, a different style of music or a new interpretation of a piece the choir has known a long time, changing the order of service for a special occasion, new ways to embody the parts of the *ordo* (a different way of greeting or praying or sending the congregation out at the end of the service). While we can be creative on our own, working with a group can exponentially magnify the possibilities.

Vulnerability

The ability to be vulnerable—showing colleagues our true self or our feelings or fears—is an invaluable element in leadership. In fact, it has been said that if we are not willing to make ourselves vulnerable, we will not be very good leaders.[11] It is fine to admit our doubts about an idea or confess hesitancy about a direction that is being considered. We might also share with colleagues a situation in which we felt insecure or a time when things just didn't go well. One musician comments on a clergy colleague:

> My pastor is a good leader. He is human. He has to deal with flaws in himself and in all of us. He makes mistakes, because he is willing to try new ways of doing things.... I think a great leader is not one who hits the bull's-eye every time, but every time, he tries to hit the bull's-eye.[12]

Leaders do not need to have all the answers, or even appear to have all the answers. This honesty and vulnerability can pay dividends in that it may encourage others' creativity beyond anyone's wildest expectations.

Accountability

As clergy and musicians, we are called to account for the ways we are fulfilling our calling as well as identifying factors that may be limiting our effectiveness. There are fundamental questions to be asked: *What has God called us to do in our lives and in this church? How do we define our ministry? What are its components and how does it fit into the overall mission of the church we are serving? How are we using our time? How are we using the available human and financial resources and opportunities?* Leaders need to be honest in their responses to these questions, as well as open to feedback from others about what is working well and what could be done more effectively.

Role Modeling

"You can effectively teach only what you consistently model. It takes one to know one, show one, and grow one,"[13] John Maxwell says. A leader's actions are constantly observed. Congregations, colleagues, and choir members—all watch our actions and listen to our words.

Clergy: Model engaged singing of the hymns or liturgy. During the anthems, resist the temptation to review your sermon notes or make "to do" lists for the coming week when you are momentarily not actively involved in leading the service. Members of the congregation are not encouraged to participate when someone visible in front of them seems to have something more important to do than to join in the liturgy.

Musicians: No silent practicing at the keyboard during the sermon and no Facebook status updates or text messaging under the pretext of a devoutly bowed head. Participate in the prayers and listen attentively to the sermon. Stay in the sanctuary during the sermon. "Why do you say that?" you ask. While leaving would never have occurred to me, I recently played at a church where members of the choir showed surprise that I had stayed in the sanctuary for the sermon at the first service and advised me that I certainly did not need to do so at the second. I said I really wanted to stay, all the while thinking to myself, "What kind of a message am I sending if I leave? That the sermon doesn't matter? Yeah, that's really good for clergy-musician relations!" I also recalled the plea of a clergy colleague, "Please, please, please tell church musicians that preachers *do not* appreciate it when the musician leaves the chancel during the sermon." I stayed.

Visionary

Effective leaders articulate a personal sense of mission and inspire others on their team to support this vision. It does not hurt if we have a certain charisma, or magnetism, that makes others want to follow us. Remember Professor Harold Hill in *The Music Man*?

Charles Kiefer and Peter Senge discuss the term *metanoic*, from a Greek word meaning "a fundamental shift of mind." The authors define a metanoic organization as one that "is based upon the principle that individuals can have extraordinary influence once aligned with a common vision. The metanoic organization embraces five primary dimensions: (1) a deep sense of vision or purposefulness; (2) alignment around that vision; (3) empowering people; (4) structural integrity; and (5) the balance of reason and intuition."[14] There is no reason that church members and staff, uniting behind a powerful, common vision, should not embody these qualities.

Sense of Humor

Humor is as essential in church work as it is in life, for that matter. People with a sense of humor are fun to be with. When we are with them, we are not only more productive, we are more collegial and have a better sense of community.

There is empirical evidence. A survey revealed that eighty-four percent of vice presidents and personnel directors in one hundred of the largest corporations in the country "felt that employees with a sense of humor are more effective on the job than people with little or no sense of humor." The study concluded that those with a sense of humor are more flexible and creative, with a greater willingness to do new things in new ways. And if that weren't enough, people with a sense of humor are more likely to be hired than those without a sense of humor.[15] Did you hear the one about …?

Life-Time Learner

As effective leaders, we maintain our skills and work to improve ourselves by staying current with journals and books, practicing, networking, attending continuing education events, setting goals and outlining ways to accomplish them. In his book *How to Thrive in Associate Staff Ministry*, Kevin Lawson observes that a majority of participants in his study not only belonged to a professional association, but also regularly attended conferences or other meetings that offered the opportunity to network, learn about others' programs, and share ideas on problem-solving:

> Over and over again, long-term associate staff members who are thriving in their ministries point to the importance of continuing education and professional enrichment. Ninety-five percent of the thriving staff members in this study identified professional growth as very important to their ability to thrive in ministry.[16]

Commitment and Consistency

Commitment is a choice that reveals the values we hold most deeply, our fundamental, core values. It is a basic quality of one's character that allows us to give our best, be our most creative, work our hardest. It is so important that Patrick Lencioni lists lack of commitment as one of *The Five Dysfunctions of a Team*.[17] Being committed demands energy and flexibility and willingness to go the second mile. We may need to meet with an additional group, offer a devotion or play for a women's guild meeting on our day off, or extend ourselves in some other significant way. That is what committed people do.

Effective leaders are also consistent; we are "on" most of the time. We have done the necessary preparation for the rehearsal, sermon, or committee meeting. Others take us at our word and they know that our work will be done well. "If you can't depend on teammates all the time," Maxwell says, "then you can't really depend on them any of the time. Consistency takes more than talent. It takes a depth of character that enables people to follow through—no matter how tired, distracted, or overwhelmed they are."[18]

Reaching out

Show Sensitivity to Language

In building a team, labels matter. Referring to colleagues as "*my* staff" is not as collegial or supportive as the term "*our* ministry team." Similarly, words like "supervisor," "subordinate" or "my report" imply hierarchy that is out of date and may be counterproductive to team-building goals. The senior pastor is "the boss," of course, but current leadership theory suggests significant value in a more collegial approach in titles as well as in process.

The imposition of such hierarchical terminology can come as a sudden and unwelcome shock to a staff accustomed to a more collegial attitude. One musician felt he was being called into the principal's office when the new pastor instituted "supervisory" sessions. It is possible that the pastor just had in mind a one-on-one staff meeting, but with that term matching the pastor's authoritarian manner, it never quite felt that way.

Treat Others with Respect

Staff members stay at a church not for the high salary but because we feel we are making a difference. We stay because we have a spiritual connection with the Gospel as it is preached and sung and enacted in this church. We stay because we are respected and so is our discipline. We stay because we are respected as colleagues, our opinions are valued, and we are able to work in harmony with other staff members. Absent these qualities, staff members may just leave, or they may remain in their job but do less excellent work because of the unsupportive environment.

When an interviewer asked a musician about what he expected from a pastor, he said, "The answer is quite simple, really. All I really want from my pastor is respect. I honestly feel that the rest will follow. That is why respect is so important. If the pastor respects the church musicians and respects their time, then agreements can be reached and things can be worked out."[19]

Staff members have a right to expect that their skills will be valued and their opinions treated with respect. Under normal working situations, we have a right to expect that our self-esteem will be protected. It is perfectly acceptable to reject the idea, but never to reject the person.

At the same time, effective leaders respect all colleagues and do not play favorites. We do not set up others to compete for our time. We do not have a favorite who gets our attention immediately (or, musicians, always gets the solos). We do not micromanage, but give ministry colleagues the authority to do their jobs as they feel called—checking in on the big items, getting feedback as appropriate, but being allowed to do their work without having someone constantly looking over their shoulder. These would all be antithetical to the spirit of humility and servant leadership that are marks of an effective leader.

Create a Positive, Fear-Free Environment

A positive environment is not only energizing, it is essential to a successful church. People prefer to work in a "can do" situation where ideas are freely offered and welcomed. It is said that people's actions are linked to affirmation. If creativity is rewarded, creative ideas flow; if new ideas are criticized, people will shut down and creative thinking will come to a screeching halt. This open environment is not only affirming for the individual, it also allows the church the benefit of each person's thinking. Staff members need to be confident that new ideas will not be immediately shot down or, worse yet, ridiculed. "People on the team," writes Maxwell, "must be made to feel that they are in an environment where it is safe to offer suggestions or criticism without feeling threatened, freely trade information in the spirit of cooperation, and discuss ideas without being negatively criticized. Open communication among teammates increases productivity."[20]

One has to be able to brainstorm and to know that ideas put on the table will be looked at fairly and, if modified, done so in a way that might make them even better. We all do our best work in an atmosphere of affirmation rather than one of criticism. As Charles Schwab wrote, "I have yet to find the [individual], however exalted ... who did not do better work and put forth greater effort under a spirit of approval than under a spirit of criticism."[21] A colleague at a large Midwestern church describes weekly meetings, dreaded by the staff, in which the senior pastor goes around the room, pointing his finger, and asking each person to account for failures (such as low attendance in choir or church school) or berating a staff member for something that did not go according to plan. Such a demeaning approach creates an environment of anxiety and tension. Staff members frequently become ill simply anticipating the next day's meeting with its tense, borderline-abusive environment. Undoubtedly the head of staff thinks that this encourages accountability, but there are other, genuinely productive ways to do that. One's best work is never done when personal attack might be the result. Even if that attack is not aimed at us, the atmosphere can be so toxic that we may just not want to continue to work there any longer.

In a fear-free environment, the working premises are: (1) we are created in the image of God and are due respect; (2) we are committed to the best interests of the church; (3) we are human and make mistakes in judgment and action. If the mistake requires an apology, we apologize; if it requires more substantial remedy, we do that as well, because we are accountable for the way we carry out our responsibilities. If the mistake requires forgiveness, we forgive. While there is an aspiration for perfection, achieving that perfection is not assumed. Have you heard the remark by English playwright and novelist W. Somerset Maugham, "Only mediocre people are always at their best!"

Show Appreciation

Someone has written, "No human being can be genuinely happy unless s/he stands well in the esteem of fellow mortals. [The person] who would deal successfully with us must never forget that we possess and are possessed by this ego.... A word of appreciation can often accomplish what nothing else could accomplish."

Here are two quite different scenarios:

1. I would like clergy to understand that in the small church (less than 200) the musician doesn't choose the seasonal cantata or large work by what he or she likes musically, or even a particular style, or mood. The competent church musician chooses what matches the forces he has been given with which to work, the amount of preparation time available, and the text or libretto of the work (not necessarily in that order). In other words, when a pastor tells you he really liked what you did this season, but you might want to consider something more upbeat next year—it's really not helpful. It's much, much more complicated than that. Can you tell that this just happened to me?[22]

2. Ron had recently come on staff at his church as worship and music pastor. The choir had been working on a particularly difficult cantata and had just presented it that Sunday evening. To Ron's trained ear, it sounded pretty good, but there were some rough spots that troubled him. When Ron arrived home later that night, the phone rang and he answered it. On the other end of the line he could hear the sound of people cheering and his pastor's voice, like an announcer at a baseball game, saying, "It's the bottom of the ninth, the home team is behind, and the bases are loaded. Ron steps up to the plate, and there's the pitch. He swings and connects. It's going, going, gone! What a massive home run! We win!" Ron cheered too and cried, and on the wave of those words of encouragement, felt deep satisfaction in the role he had taken on.[23]

Clergy: Mention your appreciation of the choir's work, the organist's dedication, or the instrumentalists' beautiful playing. This could be in the form of a mention during the service, an e-mail of appreciation, or a personal word. You might go to the choir rehearsal before the service for a time of conversation and a prayer, which would offer the opportunity to thank them for their work and affirm their role as co-leaders of worship. You might consider singing with the choir, even for a short period of time (Advent or Lent perhaps). As a former student wrote, "I was always the pastor who joined the choir right away, so I never had issues with musicians in my churches!"[24]

Musicians: It is important to show our appreciation as well. We must never fail to tell the choir what a great job they did on the previous Sunday's anthem. Similarly, tell the clergy as specifically as possible how much we appreciated the sermon, or the pace of the service, or the chanting of the liturgy. It is good to affirm our appreciation of the clergy to the choir, too, if for no other reason than to allow them to see musician and clergy as a team.

Resist the "Blame Game"

Stress fills churches these days—the stress of aging buildings and aging congregations. A recent Hartford Seminary study reports, "American congregations have grown less healthy in the past decade, with fewer people in the pews and aging memberships."[25] Overall church attendance is down and budgets are shrinking. Lovett Weems terms it an "ongoing worship recession."[26] Denominational leaders, pastors, church staffs, and lay leaders are looking for a way to stop this downward trend and turn it around. There are creative approaches to restoring the vitality of a church, re-engaging members, and attracting new people to the community. But the blame game doesn't help. Too often there's a flailing about for a quick fix: unplug the organ and unseat the organist; change the style of worship dramatically and quickly or change the style of music; blame the youth director for not doing his job in attracting youth or the Christian education program for using a dated curriculum.

Blaming individuals or programs is a dangerous tactic and a sign of an unhealthy church. It erodes trust and can severely damage the entire church community. The issues are usually complex and require prayerful consideration. The staff team and lay leadership all need to be engaged in creatively identifying these approaches together.

Show Compassion

Compassion—the ability to respond to each other with loving concern and care—is another essential quality for leadership in the church. Joyce Rupp writes in *The Cup of Our Life*, "Each life influences and affects the other in some way. The more we see our world as a vast interconnectedness of all beings, the more drawn we will be to compassion because we will see how much one life is related to and affected by another."[27] She goes on to say, "When I look at the lives of compassionate people, I see some common characteristics. They often have significant suffering or painful life events of their own, a generous heart, a non-blaming and non-judging mind, a passionate spirit, a willingness to sacrifice their life, a keen empathy, and love that embraces the oneness of all creation."[28] There is an additional aspect, the reflexive effect of compassion, which inspires us to be compassionate when we associate with people who care deeply for others. The world and the church have a critical need for people of compassion.

Share Control

Effective leaders do not attempt to go it alone and do not assume that the vision and strategies and implementation are all of their doing. "The solo leader is rarely associated with effective leadership," Weems writes.[29]

While many denominations have a heavily hierarchical staffing structure, cutting-edge leadership models these days are not hierarchical. They are "flattened," as Tom Ehrich writes in *Church Wellness: A Best Practices Guide to Nurturing Healthy Congregations.*

> Healthy organizations are "flattening" the [organizational] chart to encourage teamwork, free-flowing relationships, and individual creativity. Even traditionally pyramidal organizations like the military and corporations find that teams perform well when allowed freedom in decision-making and responding to changed circumstances. This new [approach] requires new attitudes toward power, control, and accountability, as well as heightened trust in people to function responsibly outside command-and-control structures.[30]

In building teams, leaders help staff members feel a connection with each other as well as with the overall ministry. A team is much more likely to work effectively together if there is a strong sense of community. These words from a church musician speak to this point:

> I'll admit that my entire fall has been about our stewardship theme, "Better Together" and our reading of Bonhoeffer's *Life Together,* but

> that would be my big message to both musicians and pastors: it will always be better together. Release your human need for hierarchy and talk to each other, plan together, ponder together. And don't do it all by email—look one another in the face, have lunch, pray together. You never know what you might contribute to worship in that environment.[31]

Exude Enthusiasm

We can choose to be enthusiastic or we can let our lack of enthusiasm breed negativity and diminish creativity throughout our team. Enthusiasm matters. It engenders the positive atmosphere that will ignite ministry. Staffs are synergistic, and enthusiasm is contagious. How many people have been swept along largely on the basis of a single individual's enthusiasm? Singers join choirs, congregants join mission groups, youth make sandwiches on Saturday morning to feed the homeless, all likely drawn to this work as the result of one person's enthusiasm and encouragement.

Ensure Human, System, and Financial Resources

Human resources might make sure phones are covered while the receptionist attends a staff meeting. *System resources* can ensure the bulletin is proofread multiple times to increase the chance that mistakes are caught before going to press. *Financial resources* will provide program support and salaries, as well as funds for continuing education, vacation, even compensatory time. While team members need to support each other, we also need to be able to count on support from the leadership, especially when it comes to issues of compensation. Vern Sanders writes in *Creator Magazine*: "I once had a pastor tell me 'There are two kinds of pastors: one kind takes care of themselves financially, and their staff splits up the crumbs that are left. The other kind takes care of their staff first, and trusts that they also will be taken care of.' "

The second kind are well compensated and their staff are much more loyal and productive.

Expect the Best of Others

Organizations thrive when people affirm each other and expect the best of each other. An effective leader expects the strongest commitment, the best focus, and the greatest efforts possible from colleagues. Part of expecting the best of colleagues is assessing the abilities of the group, whether a lay committee or a choir, and then challenging them just a bit. "The best musicians," writes Charlotte Kroeker, "take people just to the edge of their capabilities and then stretch them to the point where they can do it, at which point the people say, 'Wow!' It is an art to know how to do that. Frequently music leaders either take them not far enough, and you have a sort of pedantic approach, or they take them too far, and they're frustrated. An artist knows the balance."[32]

"A good leader," writes one pastor, "is someone who has learned how to read people well enough to know when to pull them, when to push them, and when you just have to get out of the way. This ability ... requires enough self-knowledge, ego strength, and selflessness to affirm others who do things well, and the willingness to let them have the credit for it."[33]

Tennis players often talk about how their game improves when they're competing with a better player. Similarly, "team members always love and admire a player who is able to help them go to another level, someone who empowers them to be successful. These kinds of people are like Boston Celtics Hall of Fame center Bill Russell, who said, 'The most important measure of how good a game I played was how much better I'd made my teammates play.' "[34]

A skilled leader looks for the special talents in others and helps them develop those talents, believing in them and encouraging them every step of the way. Lovett Weems talks about the "leader as developer," as opposed to the "leader as hero." The leader who views him/herself as a developer sees "every situation that arises as an opportunity to achieve two purposes: the accomplishment of the task and the growth and development of other people in the organization." Weems goes on to quote researchers Bradford and Cohen (*Managing for Excellence*), affirming this model because it allows leaders to "have impact without exerting total control, to be helpful without having all the answers, to get involved without demanding centrality, to be powerful without needing to dominate, and to act responsibly without squeezing others out."[35]

Take Risks

Effective leaders are willing to step out of their comfort zone, creating a positive environment where they can empower others to take risks and make changes. Risk-taking is not one of my favorite activities. Once I went up in a hot-air balloon with a choir member celebrating a birthday. I was frightened out of my mind; my fists were so tightly clenched around the rope while the balloon was in the air that it took the rest of the day to unclench them. It felt like a risk that I was proud of myself for having taken, but I don't ever intend to do that again!

The kind of risk I am talking about here is less physical, but probably no less fearful. It may involve starting a new service, initiating on-screen projection in the sanctuary when you know it will be controversial, taking the choir on tour, or starting a benefit concert series for AIDS in Africa. Risks often have a huge pay-off in terms of sense of mission, the spirit of the group, and the good that can result. The success of any new enterprise depends on the work of a team, as planning and prayer enable us, together, to "conceive, believe, achieve."

Negotiate Change

"Change" may well be one of the top ten most often-used words in books on organization and leadership. In the book *Appreciative Inquiry*, Cooperrider and Whitney talk about the customary approach to change as negative, one they call "deficit-based," whereas they recommend focusing on the "positive core." In the church, focus on the positive core means directing attention first to deeply held traditions, values, and the spirit of the congregation, as opposed to mandates issued by the leadership. Talk to people; more important, listen to them. Ask questions about what is best for the congregation and replicate others' best practices.

As churches are feeling the need to attract more members, worship styles and music are under attack from all sides. Does the choral program need to be re-energized? If so, do we need a different rehearsal schedule? A different rehearsal style? A different type of music? A new performing group? We musicians may need to stretch our levels of comfort and taste to include music that is more global or contemporary. Clergy may need to find different ways of delivering a sermon, engaging the congregation in the service, or drawing others into pastoral care.

The change may be as cosmic as re-visioning the mission of the church or as small as the institution of a fellowship hour. Whether the situation desperately needs immediate correction or we are just excited about an opportunity, involve others in the change process. It has been said, "a change imposed is a change opposed."[36] Simply put, people do not want to be changed. They certainly do not want to be manipulated or forced into change, and when that happens, they resist. Furthermore, effective leaders acknowledge that change cannot be done alone. Senge writes, "In every case I know where significant change processes have been sustained, it has been due to the workings of large numbers of people, not just isolated individuals."[37]

Let's face it: change nearly always makes people uncomfortable, as cleverly recounted in Spencer Johnson's allegory, *Who Moved My Cheese?*[38]

WHO MOVED MY CHEESE?

He reflected on the mistakes he had made in the past and used them to plan for his future. He knew that you could learn to deal with change.

You could be more aware of the need to keep things simple, be flexible, and move quickly.

You did not need to overcomplicate matters or confuse yourself with fearful beliefs.

You could notice when the little changes began so that you could be better prepared for the big change that might be coming.

He knew he needed to adapt faster, for if you do not adapt in time, you might as well not adapt at all.

He had to admit that the biggest inhibitor to change lies within yourself, and that nothing gets better until you change.

Perhaps most importantly, he realized that there is always New Cheese out there whether you recognize it at the time, or not. And that you are rewarded with it when you go past your fear and enjoy the adventure.

He knew some fear should be respected, as it can keep you out of real danger. But he realized most of his fears were irrational and had kept him from changing when he needed to.

He didn't like it at the time, but he knew that the change had turned out to be a blessing in disguise as it led him to find better Cheese.

We can't keep doing what we're doing if we don't want to keep getting what we're getting. These are challenging times, and if the church is going to "thrive, not just survive," change will undoubtedly need to happen.

Communicate Effectively

> The first service one owes to others in the fellowship consists in listening to them. Just as love of God begins in listening to His Word, so the beginning of love for the brethren is learning to listen to them. It is God's love for us that He not only gives us His Word but lends us His ear. So it is His work that we do for our brother when we learn to listen to Him.[39]
>
> —Dietrich Bonhoeffer, *Life Together*

Communication is a two-way street—listening as well as talking. Nothing is more important than listening to someone, thoughtfully and attentively. This leadership quality conveys to others that we care, the other person matters, and their ideas or feelings are worthy of consideration.

"When people don't unload their opinions and feel like they've been listened to, they won't really get on board," says Kathryn, the change agent in *The Five Dysfunctions of a Team*, adding, "most reasonable people don't have to get their way in a discussion. They just need to be heard, and to know that their input was considered and responded to."[40]

We cannot plan our next statement or look over someone's shoulder while they're talking. Instead, we actively listen to what they have to say. Part of the process of listening is feeding back, repeating what has been said in your own words, checking to make sure you have understood correctly. In Robert McCloskey's apt formulation, "I know that you believe you understand what you think I said, but I am not sure you realize that what you heard is not what I meant." Check it out with active listening.

Honor the Congregation's Story

The traditions of a congregation are important. Its history—who founded it and why, and why in this place—these are key factors in shaping the congregation. Honoring those who have been leaders in the congregation for many years is important. Ask them about the impetus behind the church's missions, how a preschool got started, why the youth program is so strong. Clergy have been known to court new members assiduously but then, implausibly, treat older members with disdain. What a mistake! We in church work are part of a continuum and a "great cloud of witnesses" preceded us; the congregation's story did not start when we arrived and it does not end when we leave. Wise leaders will embrace the story and build on it.

Music represents an important component of the congregation's story. An effective way to get to know the members of a congregation is to find out what music they like and what hymns are their favorites. One of the first things clergy and musicians would be wise to do after arriving at a new church is to meet with members in small groups and ask these questions, including reasons why specific music is especially meaningful to them. This can prove a moving experience as well as a powerful platform for bonding members with each other and with their new staff.

Seek Friendships outside the Congregation

It is important to have friends—colleagues and non-colleagues—to whom we can pour out our hearts and who will listen lovingly to our frustrations. These friends need to be people who will give us honest feedback and be willing to tell us when our take on a situation may not be the right one. Meet for coffee, meet for prayer. Whatever the venue, consider this an investment in your sanity and your effectiveness in ministry.

Pray

Effective leaders have an active personal prayer life, and this extends to their immediate communities as well. They not only pray for other staff members, they pray with them; they pray for their health and families, and they pray for their church and for those to whom they minister. This is a crucial component in maintaining connection with each other, and to keeping all connected with their calling, their ministry, and God.

Notes

1. Greenleaf, 352.

2. *Ibid.*, 27.

3. *Ibid.*, 12.

4. Charlotte Kroeker, *The Sounds of Our Offerings: Achieving Excellence in Church Music,* Herndon, VA: Alban Institute, 2011, 186.

5. Roberts, 34.

6. Larson and LaFasto, 128.

7. Kroeker, 149.

8. Nouwen, 9.

9. *Ibid.*, 22–23.

10. James C. Collins, *Good to Great: Why Some Companies Make the Leap ... and Others Don't,* New York: HarperCollins, 2001, 13.

11. Greenleaf, 356–357.

12. Kroeker, 20.

13. John Maxwell, *The 17 Essential Qualities of a Team Player: Becoming the Kind of Person Every Team Wants,* Nashville: Thomas Nelson, 2002, xii.

14. Larson and LaFasto, 119.

15. http://www.laughterremedy.com/articles/corporate_perceptions.html, accessed February 25, 2012.

16. Lawson, 46–47.

17. Patrick Lencioni, *The Five Dysfunctions of a Team: A Leadership Fable,* San Francisco: Jossey-Bass, 2002.

18. Maxwell, *The 17 Essential Qualities of a Team Player,* 52.

19. Becky Torres, paper for Wesley Chapel Choir, December 11, 2011.

20. Maxwell, *Teamwork 101,* 63.

21. Maxwell, *The 17 Essential Qualities of a Team Player,* 66.

22. John David Horman, e-mail to author, October 4, 2011.

23. Lawson, 23.

24. Chris Weitzel, e-mail to author, October 16, 2011.

25. http://www.washingtonpost.com/national/on-faith/church-attendance-down-congregations-getting-older-report-says/2011/09/29/gIQA7jjvAL_story.html, accessed February 25, 2012.

26. *Leading Ideas,* Lewis Center for Church Leadership, e-mail newsletter, September 7, 2011.

27. Joyce Rupp, *The Cup of Our Life: A Guide for Spiritual Growth,* Notre Dame: Ave Maria Press, 2004, 110.

28. *Ibid.,* 114.

29. Lovett H. Weems, Jr., *Church Leadership: Vision, Team, Culture, and Integrity,* Rev. ed., Nashville: Abingdon Press, 2010, 59.

30. Tom Ehrich, *Church Wellness: A Best Practices Guide to Nurturing Healthy Congregations,* New York: Church Publishing Incorporated, 2008, 43–44.

31. Susan Sevier, e-mail to author, October 7, 2011.

32. Kroeker, 149–150.

33. *Ibid.,* 169.

34. Maxwell, *The 17 Essential Qualities of a Team Player,* 66.

35. Weems, 72–73.

36. Spencer Johnson, *Who Moved My Cheese? An A-mazing Way to Deal with Change in Your Work and in Your Life,* New York: G. P. Putnam's Sons, 1998, 81.

37. Greenleaf, 359.

38. Johnson, 72–73

39. Dietrich Bonhoeffer, *Life Together,* tr. Daniel W. Bloesch and James H. Burtness, Minneapolis, Fortress Press, 2004, 98.

40. Lencioni, 94–95.

4
Effective Musicians: Qualities and Skills

Every musician I know would like to have these words said to or about them: "I am so grateful for all of the musicians with whom I have worked. Their musical offerings have ministered to me at countless unexpected moments. I could not do ministry without them."

—Barb Kenley, e-mail to author

The skills needed to be an effective church musician are numerous and varied. Musicians may be among the original life-time learners, because we never stop learning and growing throughout our careers. Whether part-time or full-time, volunteer or well-compensated, choir director, organist, or both, we musicians must develop and maintain certain skills if we are to be successful in our work.

Develop a Philosophy of Church Music

Effective musicians will have a cogent, spiritually-grounded, and thoughtfully-articulated theology of music's role in the church, particularly in worship. We may be asked to share these views in the interview process, and once on staff, we should engage with ministerial colleagues, the worship committee, choirs, and congregation in further refining these ideas as they relate to the particular church. To enable members of the congregation to grow in their appreciation for music and its power to influence their spirits and their lives, the following ideas should be shared on retreats and in small group settings.

Show that We Appreciate the Way God Speaks to Us through Music

We need to share our thoughts about the power of music and how it can be used in the service, and articulate reasons why a particular piece of music is chosen and the reasons why it fits best in a particular place. Music has the power to motivate, convey emotions, paint pictures, promote healing, and build community. Most important, music tells the story of God's work in human history and the story of salvation. Artful choices of music for the service involve sensitivity to the moment: does the moment call for a piece of some complexity (a Howells anthem or a Bach motet) or something simpler (a piece that is without textual or harmonic challenges)? Some occasions call for stretching the ears and spirits of both congregation and choir; at other times we need to choose music that is simple, familiar, and loved.

Uphold the Congregation as the Church's Most Important Choir

This might sound strange to those of us who spend our careers developing a fine choral program, but it is important to realize that the primary role of a choir is to encourage the congregation's worship. While the choir may sometimes perform on behalf of the congregation, their primary role is enabling and supporting the sung prayer and praise of the congregation itself. Perhaps the choir sits mixed with members of the congregation at some services (a wonderful way to encourage the congregation's full participation in the singing), introduces new hymns by singing a verse or two before the congregation joins on later verses, or sings verses with the congregation singing the refrain. They are not there to entertain or take the place of the congregation. The choir is there to lead the congregation in worship.

Embrace Music as a Sacred Treasure

The music of the church is truly a treasure, and a beloved piece of music is one of many jewels in the box of musical treasures. To sing chant, the songs of the early Reformers, the frontier camp meeting, the urban revivals, or spirituals and gospel music connects us with an earlier time and place in the history of the church. We take pride in explaining a treasure in our homes—how we got it, who owned it before, and why it means something special to us. We guard and preserve it so that it can be passed down to our children or our grandchildren. It is the same with sacred music.

Educate the Congregation

Music notes in the bulletin that give information about the music enrich the congregation's understanding of the music. Occasionally, such comments might be offered during the service itself, which would not only convey information about the music, but also the musician's enthusiasm for it. When a musician offers comments during the service, the congregation—often more familiar with the back of our heads than our faces—gets to know us a bit better.

Choirs Aren't a Democracy

While collegiality and consultation are vital, the undisputable fact is, as Thomas Are explains, "The choir remains one organization in the church that must be run by a dictator. The democratic process is too cumbersome to function during a rehearsal. Individuals cannot take a vote on which pitch they want to sing or what tempo they will follow. The director is boss."[1] Decisions on musical selection and interpretation have to be made by the director, but, that said, the focus must be on how the music serves the needs of the assembly, not on our infallible musical sensibility. While it is a fine idea to ask the choir from time to time "Does that feel too fast?" or "How about we try it this way and see what we think," the ultimate decision belongs to the director.

Mentor Others

Most of us were mentored by choir directors or teachers, and it is appropriate that we share our wisdom and enthusiasm with those who might follow in our footsteps. Relish the opportunity to encourage children and youth to share their musical gifts with church school classes and in services. Arrange for them to be involved in the music program in other meaningful ways, from anthem filing to inviting older singers to conduct a younger choir. Some larger churches have interns or apprentices who volunteer (or are paid modestly) in order to get hands-on experience. Have "share the bench" Sundays where children are invited to sit on the organ bench. After the service, offer organ demonstrations for congregants of any age who would like to know more about the organ and how it does what it does. Depending on schedules and church policy, organists might offer lessons to pianists who would like to learn to play the organ. At the very least, the church should make its instruments available for students to practice.

Church musicians are a conduit, offering a way for people to connect with each other and with God.

"Performance" Is Not a Bad Word

Work to differentiate between a performance that highlights the skills of the performer and one that draws attention to God. "Those who effectively 'perform' their role do so with such a combination of skill and integrity that worshipers do not focus upon the leader, but are drawn into a transforming relationship with God."[2]

Church musicians are a conduit, offering a way for people to connect with each other and with God. It is an awesome opportunity in the truest sense of that word. As musicians, we must guard against conveying the sense that we are the most important part of the service. While most musicians do not feel that way, others may judge us to have the motive of self-aggrandizement. Often the better we are, the more we are thought to be just performing. It can be dangerous to project intent on someone else, but it happens, especially when a congregation does not know the musician very well. In such instances, clergy can support the musician by clarifying their common understanding role of music in the service. Dr. David McAllister-Wilson, president of Wesley Theological Seminary, speaks to this:

> Musicians should be able to think theologically but I also think they should think pastorally, meaning, knowing what the pastoral moment is in history and in the life of a particular congregation. They need to have the whole picture of the service in mind. These qualities they share with the clergy. The things the musician brings are: the language of music, which is different from the language of the rest of the liturgy; and attention to quality "performance" (yes, I mean that word). The musician can bring the values of virtuosity and performance to the rest of the service. In this way, the whole service can learn from a good piece of music about things like pace, timing, transitions. A service ought to be like a symphony with themes and movements.[3]

Know the Congregation

Get a sense of the unwritten rules on issues like friendships in the congregation—are they encouraged? Strongly discouraged? I know of churches that have claimed that friendships with members of the congregation were not allowed, yet it happened all the time. The flip side of this issue is research showing that people who thrive in ministry testify that "their friendships with members of their congregations were a strong source of support that helped them thrive in ministry."[4] Congregations differ in size, number of staff members, and culture—all of which are important variables—and the wise musician gets a sense of the advisability of friendships within the church early on.

Help the Church Recognize Its Program Needs

Church committees often have only the vaguest ideas as to what the role of the musician can be in their community. They need help in discerning the kind of program they want, what a church musician actually does, and what compensation is appropriate for the time the church desires and the education and experience the musician brings to the position.

Paul Westermeyer writes, "Since the educational institutions of the church generally do such a poor job of training people for the role of the church musician or preparing pastors or churches to understand that role, one cannot expect churches to be aware of what they need. It is only when they wrestle with these issues that they realize what is required."[5] The websites of the American Guild of Organists and many denominations have guidelines for job descriptions and contracts. These can help a church realize that the program it wants may require more time and compensation than they had anticipated.

Technical Skills

Self-Discipline

The musician is probably already disciplined. If not, he or she would likely not be holding a job as a church musician. Musicians cannot develop keyboard skills without hours and hours of practice. The same goes for choral work as one develops the singers' breath support and vocal control, learns how to rehearse effectively, and discovers ways to elicit from a choir the sound that a particular piece requires. Yes, inspiration and sometimes spontaneity can be involved in making music. It also takes a lot of discipline.

Organization

Church music programs require significant organization of people and materials: the music library needs to be organized and catalogued if it is not already; octavos arriving monthly need to be read through or categorized so they can be located again when needed; organ music, piano music, music for instrumental ensembles or praise bands all need to be filed. (Piles in the corner don't count!) In addition, a music program means coordinating many people, sometimes in multiple ensembles. Rehearsal times and performance schedules can be complex. Even a small group requires a fair amount of organization.

In addition, church musicians must coordinate with the clergy since sermon and scripture information guides music choices much of the time. In turn, music information needs to be in the hands of the person who prepares the bulletin or screen projections in a timely manner.

Part of being organized and disciplined is honoring the time and talents of others. A musician writes:

> I think respect for the time of others is critical. All of my rehearsals begin exactly when I say they'll begin, and they end at the time they're scheduled to end. If I find I really need more rehearsal time, I tell them the week prior that "next week's rehearsal is going to go ten or fifteen minutes longer." That's the only way I'll extend rehearsals. So, respect for their time means organization on my part.[6]

Connect with All the Church's Musicians

Effective musicians are in regular contact with other musicians, including singers, instrumentalists, the praise team, and anyone we see regularly. Many musicians send Monday morning e-mails to thank people for the weekend's work and to cheer them on for upcoming music. A good way to keep in touch is through a sign-out calendar so the director knows when an absence is expected and thus whether that double-choir anthem is possible after all. An unexpected absence from a rehearsal or two merits a follow-up personal e-mail, note, or phone call to let them know they were missed, check if everything is OK, or ask if there is a pastoral emergency they would want shared with others.

Value the Talent of Others as Well as Your Own

Many congregations have lots of talented musicians, although some may be too shy or feel too rusty to let their talents be known. Take it as a sacred obligation to use the talents of congregational members to the best of your ability and the best of their willingness to share their talent.

Musicians need to schedule practice time, rehearsal preparation time, personal devotion time, social time, and down time. Always meet deadlines and never succumb to "I'm an artist" as an excuse for missing them. Church musicians are notorious for saying yes to every opportunity, not only to be seen as supportive of the ministry but also because they love doing what they do. This super-willingness can draw down the finite energy every person has for the most important tasks.

Exercise Diplomacy

There are both good and not-so-good ways one can ask for a change of sound in the choir. I really did hear one director growl, "Sopranos, you sound like you've been gargling with a drain cleaner!" It was not said as a joke and it did not get the desired results. Diplomacy will always be our best friend and will also keep people singing in our choirs.

Use Humor

A sense of humor goes a long way. I'm not talking about doing stand-up comedy during the rehearsal, but off-hand comments that lighten the mood. I often joke that "I'm paying extra for ending consonants tonight," or "well, that was practically perfect" when we had just read through the music for the first time and it was a disaster—all said teasingly and with a smile. Choirs want to do well and they know that the director has worked hard at choosing music that matches their ability and is also a good fit in a particular context or service. A light touch can encourage their extra effort. Singers come to rehearsal for lots of reasons—some spiritual, some musical. Another reason is to have a good time, and they should not leave choir rehearsal without having had at least one good chuckle.

Expand Competency

As church musicians, we know what we are doing at the keyboard, and we very likely are also skilled conductors of instrumentalists and choirs. Not only do we need to know the basic repertoire of sacred music—the breadth of the congregational song from chant to contemporary praise choruses—we also need to know pieces that range from the demanding to those that can be sung with a skeletal group on a "down Sunday" (like the Sunday after Thanksgiving or Christmas).

My experience has been that global music (instrumental and vocal) can enhance worship by adding textures and sounds that may well move someone more than the repertoire from the Western European/American canon. We live in a wonderful era in which there are many opportunities to expand our knowledge base first-hand—through events sponsored by professional organizations such as the American Guild of Organists, the American Choral Directors Association, Chorister's Guild, and denominational organizations. These events may be one evening, one day, or week-long experiences. They are not only replete with new repertoire and performance practices, but they also provide the inspiration and support so necessary for our ministry.

Worship Planning Skills

Acquire Familiarity with Theological Language

Church musicians need to be sufficiently familiar with theological language to have meaningful conversations with the clergy. It means so much when people speak our native language—even a little of it! I know only a few phrases of Korean, but Korean students are enormously appreciative whenever I talk to them in their language. The same goes for theological language. It is essential to be able to talk about the beliefs of our denomination, church history, the Bible, or Christian formation in a way that allows us to be accepted as a peer and a colleague by the clergy. (In Chapter 5, I recommend that clergy learn musical terminology.)

Know the Liturgical Year

Know what the journey through the liturgical seasons is all about, as well as the hymns, anthems, and other music that support this journey. There are many denominational resources both online and in print to give ideas that can be merged with the culture of our congregation, the spirit of the particular service, and the ability of the choir.

Appreciate the Value of Repetition

Being a slave to innovation can be a trap. In my first decades as a church musician, and as a pretty creative person, I felt that I had an obligation to share that creativity with congregations. More recently, however, I have come to realize the value of repetition, of allowing people to sing a piece often enough for it to become music of their heart. This may mean singing the same music in different ways over a number of weeks, or singing it several weeks in succession. Repetition is important and appreciated. In an era with so much spiritual searching, we are giving our congregations a great gift by encouraging the same song until they can sing it from the heart.

The repetition concept also applies to major festivals. How many of us have used particular carol arrangements on Christmas Eve for years and had that practice reinforced by returning college students who tell you how they can't wait for that service and how much they look forward to hearing that music again. That music may have been part of their life in the church for a long time and it represents a musical homecoming for them.

Demonstrate Sensitivity to the Way Music Fits into the Service

Music is a wonderful vehicle that has been called "portable theology." It allows the congregation to take with them the point of the sermon or a key scripture passage. It is well known that music greatly assists in memorization and in conveying themes and thoughts. But the service isn't just about the music. The music needs to be integrated into the fabric of the service so that the elements of Gathering, Proclamation, Response, and Sending Forth unfold synergistically in a way that produces a profound worship experience.

Display Creativity

The true artist shows a willingness to do old things in new ways and explore new ideas as well. We must be willing to take risks, whether it means finding a new text for the Doxology for a season, trying a new placement of the choir, incorporating percussion instruments with music from around the world, singing in new languages, or just breaking out of "the way we have always done it" (whatever *it* is). Musicians are often the most creative people on a church staff. The possibilities are virtually endless; any limits are self-imposed.

One of those limits is fear—fear of not being perfect, or of failing to perform the music exactly the way it would be in its country of origin, or of dishonoring it by not performing it correctly. In my experience, any faithful effort is an honorable one. Faithful effort means doing the homework required to find the performance practice, pronunciation, percussion patterns, perhaps even the physical movement appropriate to the piece. Faithful effort also involves devising a technique of teaching the music to the choir and congregation that allows them to experience this music fully.

Finally, make sure to bring the rest of the staff into thinking on these new music choices, along with choirs and the worship planning group. Building understanding and "buy-in" increases the chances of success.

Appreciate the Gift of Leading a Congregation in Song

Leading a congregation's worship is one of the great honors and joys in the life of a church musician. Putting prayers and songs on the lips of those in the congregation—prayers and songs that they will take out of the service with them—is an amazing opportunity.

We have already mentioned the way hymnody (and to some extent any music sung in worship) constitutes "portable theology." The music can enable worshipers to take the message with them as they leave the service. Here is an example of that. One Sunday some years ago, the chair of the board of trustees at the church where I was serving came up to me before the service and said, pretty sternly, "Eileen, I'm really mad at you." Now, there are certain people in any congregation that you *never* want mad at you, and for me, the chair of the board of trustees is one of them. In my most pastoral manner, I asked her to please "tell me more." She responded, "You know that hymn we sang last week—the one that goes 'What does the Lord require of you?' Well, I haven't been able to get it out of my head all week!" I'm thinking to myself, "Praise the Lord! It's not a bad thing for someone to be singing the powerful text of Micah 6:8 *all week!*"

Recognize the Choir's Multiple Purposes to Prepare, Respond *and* Proclaim

While music is often thought of as a way to prepare people to hear the Word, it does more than that. Music can also be a response to the Word as it is read or preached, and it can be the principal vehicle for the proclamation itself. Music in the service may often include the exact text of the scriptures or be a reflection on it. The music sung by the choir is, ideally, a statement of their faith, articulating at the same time aspirations for the ways all in worship can—that very week—make a difference in the world. This ability to impact the countless parishioners who hear the choir week after week is a true gift. The text John Bell uses in the hymn, "The Summons," comes to mind: "Will you use the faith you've found to reshape the world around?"[7] Just as Martin Luther proclaimed that "music is a fair and glorious gift of God," the opportunity to share music with one's congregation is itself also a precious gift.

Embrace a Pastoral as Well as a Musical Role

Balance Pastoral and Musical Roles

Musicians have more than just a musical role; they have a pastoral relationship with those who fall within their area of ministry. This can be delicate because, while some clergy encourage this relationship, others are threatened when non-clergy exercise pastoral roles such as visiting choir members in the hospital or lending a supportive ear. Some musicians may not be entirely comfortable with the pastoral role, whether leading the choir in prayer or making hospital calls.

To them, I say I don't think one can be a church musician without caring about the whole person. Thus I encourage working through that discomfort in order to be a *pastoral* as well as a musical presence in the congregation.

"Nobody is born a pastor," says William Bradley Roberts. "The role is acquired through life experiences, education, and prayer. Clergy may find themselves working with a musician, part-time or full-time, for whom incorporating the role of pastor into music ministry is a strange notion. Keeping the larger picture in mind, however, transformation is the very nature of the church's enterprise—transformation not only among the church's members, but also within its leadership."[8] The way musicians view themselves can be transformed through the support and encouragement of colleagues in ministry.

Minister of Music and Pastoral Musician are two among various titles that can describe this role. While a pastoral title might not be an equally comfortable fit for everyone—we are, after all, not clergy, but musicians—such a title carries with it possibilities that can mean a lot as we move beyond the strictly musical components of our responsibilities and approach the people of the congregation in a more broadly spiritual way.

One afternoon a young woman in the choir came to me to say she was an alcoholic and asked if I would be willing to go with her to an AA meeting. Later that same evening another singer came to tell me that he was gay, coming out of the closet and leaving his wife and two children. At that point my thought was: "Hey, they didn't cover *this* in music school!" So I found myself going back to graduate school, taking courses in pastoral counseling. Although I still do not feel equipped to do actual pastoral counseling, at least I know how to listen more effectively, and how to steer people to those who are in a position to help.

In *Faithsong*, Thomas Are says "The most important quality a minister of music can bring to the task is a love for people. Love and concern for people must come through for sacred music to have integrity."[9]

Musicians can feel a sense of pastoral calling just as clergy do. Speaking of the church musician as a transformational leader, Hugh Ballou writes, "God calls the church musician and those skilled in ministry through music, not as an end in itself, but as a means to a greater end—forming Christian faith through all we do.... The church musician—the conductor of the choir, the music leader for worship—must be focused on and dedicated to leading people in a strong spiritual journey through liturgy and worship participation.... The conductor is, in fact, a spiritual leader, a transformational leader empowered by God."[10]

Feed Our Spiritual Needs

It can be difficult having one's place of work also be one's primary faith community. If, as a musician, we cannot worship as we play or conduct, or if the environment is too politically-loaded to do so, find another place for spiritual nourishment. Keep a journal, form a prayer group with colleagues, or seek spiritual direction. Regardless of the means, keeping a life of faith fed is an important part of effectiveness in ministry.

If a musician is not serving in his/her own denomination, Paul Westermeyer offers these suggestions: have a sense of your own faith, knowledge of the beliefs of the congregation one is serving, and an ability to "enter with empathy into their experience."[11]

Know Ourselves

Most of us are not equally good at the various skills a position may require. We may be stronger at choral conducting and weaker in our work with praise bands, or more comfortable with organ masterpieces and less with gospel piano. What do we do really well? Do we need to involve others or upgrade our own skills? "You must learn to look inward and discover your true identity and your essential gifts before attempting to impact the lives of other people," writes Hugh Ballou.[12]

Accept Personal Limitations

Musicians need to accept the fact that we will never read all we could read about music, we will never know all the rehearsal techniques, and we will never have every effective choral warm-up at our fingertips. Likewise, we will never be able to examine all the anthems that come in the mail regularly, nor will we know all the performance practices of various genres of music, nor all the ways music can engage the congregation in worship. We are finite! As Westermeyer states, "There is always something new to learn, something new to do, a new hymn, a new anthem, a new harmonization, a new skill, a new insight, a new tone color or tempo, something stimulating that suggests another way to understand and express the song. Life-long learning is built into the [church musician's] responsibility— learning as varied as the designs of a kaleidoscope."[13]

Clarify Roles when Necessary

In the absence of clarity, wise musicians work to get that clarity for themselves and others with whom they work. Silence may be golden in some situations, but this is not one of them. It is necessary that we be clear on our role as a worship and ministerial leader. Westermeyer writes passionately about the need for clarity of our role, asking if we are merely music grinders or entertainers, or if our role in the church and in worship is one that is more profound.

> We live in a culture in which musicians can find excellent technical training, but the unspoken presupposition is always that musicians are entertainers. The nature of the entertainment may vary widely, from symphony orchestra to opera to rock concert, to dance hall to popular recordings to television commercials and elevator music. Some of this music may be called edifying rather than entertaining, and some of it may be considered trivial. But the church musician as church musician (not concert artist or performer) doesn't really fit any of these categories and can easily begin to feel like a second-class citizen.[14]

Yes, we are working from a disadvantage. According to Thomas Are,

> Church musicians are the most neglected of all professionals. They are crowded into an all-too-small rehearsal room, given an all-too-small budget, an enormous task, and lots of "good lucks."
>
> They often fail! We wonder why.
>
> Many denominations have no office or officer committed to helping local choir directors do a better job. Each congregation, left to its own resources, reaches out into the community to bring in the best leadership it can find. Some churches do very well. Others, desperate for a musician, will hire almost anyone who can beat out a melody on the piano. Preparation for the ministry of music may involve little more than playing trombone in the college band; but if one can handle "Come to Jesus" in the key of C, a position as director of the music program of the local church may be waiting. Even so, when such persons fail, it is often not because of poor musicianship but because of role confusion.[15]

Some of us work in famous churches with fine instruments, fine choirs, and a generous budget—but others are often part-time, without adequate salary and sometimes without adequate respect. It's often said, "Show me your budget and I'll show you your priorities." When the musician is part-time, another job is probably getting the bulk of that person's time and energy. Clarity is essential in this situation, because the church may expect more of the musician's time than can be given while juggling other jobs necessary to keeping the mortgage paid. If the church wants more of the musician's time because they want to add more choirs or increase the number of services, the church will need to compensate the musician for these expanded duties.

Build Community in Your Musical Ensembles

Musicians may wish to incorporate prayer and/or a time of devotions into choir rehearsals, recognizing the importance of forming a spiritual community within the choir. There are many choral groups in many towns in which a singer can sing, if that's all he or she cares about. Singing in a church choir involves much more; it involves creation of a spiritual community. Sharing of prayer concerns can take substantial time, and to allow for that, one may need to give up some polishing or note learning in order to have enough time for prayer. Of course, these spiritual moments need to be handled with sensitivity according to the faith tradition in which one is serving.

Here, as recounted by William Bradley Roberts, is an example of how a choir can develop into a spiritual community:

> A number of years ago, when I had just begun work in a new parish, a long-standing member of the choir's bass section approached me with the blustery admonition, "You know, we don't come here to pray. We come to sing".... We continued to pray in these choir rehearsals, and in the case of the blustery bass, praying together was something that he either adapted to, or else learned to put up with. Eventually members of this choir became a spiritual community to each other, something that nearly always happens after people begin to pray together. When someone in the choir was sick or going through a crisis, it became entirely natural after a time for others in the group to extend a caring hand. Sometimes I, the leader, didn't even know when such acts of charity occurred. They simply became natural among the choir. Another joyful outcome of this increased intimacy was extraordinary parties. People who come to love each other not only care for one another, but they also enjoy being together.[16]

Group-building exercises in rehearsal and retreats can be valuable. Choirs that become communities, with members who genuinely care about each other and hold each other in prayer, sing better together because it emanates from a core of integrity. "We can perform better because we have experienced as well as proclaimed the gospel of grace and acceptance," one singer said. "The church choir that becomes an example of its message has something genuine to sing."[17] Choir singers have a need to feel a sense of belonging. They want to know they are accepted, contributing to the group, and more broadly, to the ministry of music in the church. The bond of singing draws people together and allows them to feel that they are contributing musically and spiritually to a whole that is much greater than the sum of the parts. Those particular singers will never again experience that music in the same way.

Remain Aware of Demands on Colleagues, Especially the Clergy

Churches are complex social organizations. Being aware of particular demands on others at stressful times of the church year as well as normal times is the mark of a good colleague.

> There is no way to write a job description for a preacher, but certain things are obvious. First of all, Tom is a manager. His church is nearly as busy as an international airport—Sunday school, kindergarten, youth programs, women's organizations, special services, and what seems like millions of committee meetings—and Tom manages it all. He monitors one of the busiest telephones in town. He administers a budget of thousands of dollars. He spends hours reading to keep up with what's going on in the world, the community, his own denomination, new trends in theology, psychology, and current ministries of the church. He makes endless visits on prospects, the sick, those in crisis, members in hospitals, and shut-ins. Also, there are those calls just to keep in touch.[18]

Clergy have a tough job. They are considered to be on call 24/7—and as servant leaders they may respond willingly to parishioner crises at any hour of the day or night, as well as other pastoral needs. "I hate to bother you" (this late at night … on a Saturday … when you're already home) is a phrase that clergy hear often. Again, the stress of always being "on" can take its toll, and musicians can provide support at particularly demanding times in the life of the clergy just as we should be able to look to colleagues for support at stressful times in our lives.

Acknowledge that We Won't Please Everyone

Remember the story about an organist who talked about four people coming up to him at the organ console after the service? One of them said he had been playing too loud and the congregation's singing was drowned out; another said the organ had been too soft and the congregation needed more support. The next pair also brought opposing reviews: the hymns were too fast for one, too slow for the other. And they were all right! Each of them experienced the music in a different way, according to their personal temperaments, their mood, even the barometric pressure. We do not need to defend ourselves by saying "I'm playing slower than the last organist," or "I'm playing louder today because last week people complained it was too soft." We simply thank them for caring enough to share their thoughts.

We all want to please our parishioners and we know that we will never fully succeed even as we keep trying. We accept the elusive goal of finding a balance between our musical training and convictions and the desire to please the congregation.

Recognize Weaknesses and the Resulting Insecurities

A musician colleague was understandably very insecure because he was not at all a good conductor. Whenever an instrumentalist playing for him made a mistake (like coming in at the wrong time), it was nearly always the conductor's fault because he wasn't clear or didn't know what he wanted in the first place. As the saying goes with conducting, "what they see is what you get." But this conductor would heap criticism on the orchestral musicians so caustically that eventually no one in town would play for him. His bravado mask did not serve him, the music, or the congregation well. If he had approached the orchestra as partners rather than adversaries, they would have been able to make great music together. Sadly, that did not happen.

There are other reasons for our insecurity. We may feel inadequate because we have had little conducting training, we're really choir-directors-drafted-to-play-the-organ, we have had no theological training, or because we are traumatized by technology. The answer to these insecurities is to admit our weaknesses and then get the training to develop the skills!

Show Appreciation to Others

It's absolutely critical to acknowledge the dedication of the members of the choir, the extra rehearsals they have attended, or the fundraising they have undertaken for new choir robes. We can't overlook the extra hours spent by the brass ensemble, the choir librarian, those who care for the robes or who arrange the chairs in the sanctuary for the instrumental ensemble. Equally essential is acknowledging staff colleagues. Bottom-line: one can really never say thank you too often.

Avoid Misuse of Power

Musicians are often perceived as having a certain amount of power. They have a prominent role in a congregation for several reasons. One is the powerful role music can play in the life of a singer or member of the congregation. Another may be the length of time the musician has been in ministry with a particular congregation. Musicians who direct a wide range of choirs from elementary to high school may well have been involved in a child's life from kindergarten to high school graduation, and this may extend further to include baptisms and weddings. Such long-term relationships can give musicians an unparalleled opportunity to minister to families in times of joy and times of crisis over many years. Particular care is needed in situations where a musician has acquired a degree of prominence in a congregation that can provide opportunities for the exercise of power. Power-brokering is never a good idea, and tempting as it might be to have a friendly conversation about the new handbell tables you need with the head of the finance committee who sings bass in the choir, it is never appropriate to abuse one's power in this way. Hear this from the perspective of a clergywoman:

> A paid musician and his/her family members should not be allowed to get into offices of the church where they potentially can become major power wielders. Musicians should be watched very carefully if it becomes obvious to the pastor that their styles tend to involve trying to exert much influence over the overall direction of church ministry and decision processes through their carefully cultivated friendships with chief behind the scenes power brokers and/or through participation in the confidential conversations outside the public forums and meetings where the ministry of the church should be discussed.[19]

Conversely, a music colleague writes, "In my situation, I did resign and left with dignity, knowing that I could have, with just a few well-placed telephone calls, exerted the power that I had gathered in the life of the church as a long-term staff member. I also knew that, ultimately, it would hurt the church more than solve the problem if I exerted that power."[20]

Display Professionalism in Communications

This means that one never forwards e-mails to a third party without first getting permission. It means never saying unflattering things about members of your staff or congregation on a social media site or a blog, and it means not writing or forwarding crude jokes or pornography. It also means never coming to a rehearsal, meeting, or church service inebriated. Why am I writing this? Sad to say, musicians have done all of these things and, not surprisingly, they no longer are employed by their churches. Churches are becoming sensitive to communications issues within their congregations and may have already developed guidelines or policies that all personnel are expected to observe.

Avoid Becoming Easily Discouraged

While there may be many other churches that deserve our talent, and while we may be fed up with the egotistical staff member who seems to be unmercifully critical and bent on making our lives miserable, it is still important to step back, evaluate the plusses and minuses, and seek counseling or mediation before resigning. Having said that…

Know when It's Time to Leave

Sometimes it just does not work. We need to know when we and the job are no longer a fit. The chapter on conflict deals with situations that lead one to the conclusion that it's just not working. For now, hear the words of Paul Westermeyer:

> If you as the church musician are pushed around by a manipulative pastor, or, if one family in the church starts to control your choice of music, you have a bad compromise or no compromise at all. You cannot contribute your talents in such a situation because you are again reduced to being a music grinder or hired chattel. Even if you analyzed the fit as carefully as possible before you came, you may early or late discover that you did not analyze well enough. You may have to leave. You do not do this lightly, you do not do it without face-to-face discussions and meetings, and you do it with deep regret. But do it you must so that you can move to a place where serving the Lord and serving the people is possible.[21]

What Clergy Want Musicians to Know

What do you, as clergy, want church musicians to know?

What do you want them do to as part of a ministerial team?

I posed these two questions to clergy colleagues from a variety of denominations. Their answers:

Thomas Troeger
Episcopal priest and Presbyterian minister
Lantz Professor of Christian Communication
Yale Divinity School and Institute of Sacred Music, New Haven, Connecticut
National Chaplain, American Guild of Organists

I want musicians to understand the profound pastoral and theological dimensions of the art of music used in the worship of God at the same time that I want them to be excellent in the practice of their craft.

William Bobby McClain
Mary Elizabeth Joyce Professor of Preaching and Worship
United Methodist minister
Wesley Theological Seminary, Washington, D.C.

During my more than fifty years in the ministry of the church, I have worked with literally scores of church musicians, or better, musicians who worked with churches—and there is a real difference. I have served as senior pastor of four churches in different sections of the United States, served twice as chair of national committees to produce hymnals for the church, as a consultant to a number of hymnal committees, and as co-teacher in seminary courses on music and worship. But I have never been asked to respond to the question that the writer of this book has asked of me. I am sure I have thought about it, but never in a systematic way, and I certainly have never written those thoughts down to be published and read by others. So let me do it now.

I offer these reflections from the perspective of a senior pastor, but I also am looking at it from a larger perspective: as seminary professor, and as one who leads worship and preaches in many places, in churches of many denominations, and one who appreciates the music of the church—past and present—as joining voices and instruments to praise God and to extend the grace of God to all creation.

1. The pastor and the musician are a team and must work together as a team to create an environment of sound that informs and enhances the worship of God. While musical knowledge and skills to play an instrument (or the use of the voice) are

involved, it is a service of worship and not a class or a performance. It is a congregation gathered around the Word and the Sacraments and not an audience to be entertained. The objective ought to be to please the One worshiped and receive the applause from that Source rather than from "an audience gathered" seeking pleasure. This basic understanding is paramount to everything else that informs the team and its work together.

2. Congregational singing is at the heart of worship and should be taken seriously in planning worship. While I love the wonderful classical music of the great composers (I sang the recitatives and arias of Handel's *Messiah* in the college choir when I was once a tenor!), it is through singing that the congregation responds to God's call and the people are able to express their faith and unite their voices with others in praising and worshiping God and offering God's grace to all of creation. Good planning and good choir practice can enhance this act of worship. As a pastor I often attended rehearsal and certainly was glad to do so when the musicians asked me to come—sometimes to help give some clarity and help focus the anthems and other music for some obscure sermon title I had announced ahead of time. All of the music and everything else throughout the service should be a response to God's Word.

3. There ought to be order but flexibility in the worship. Both pastor and musician should be thoroughly familiar with the basic pattern of worship of the denomination and the local church tradition, but also should be open to the Spirit's movement. I still believe that God can surprise us sometimes in worship! I do not in any way mean helter-skelter and trivial additions to prolong the service, but a genuine openness to the power of the Holy Spirit. There should be a standard for impact [and the "building up of the community"] rather than shock. Even the "Spirit" must be "tested, whether it is of God ..." [I John 4:1] This ought to be discussed by the team early in their work together.

4. Diversity of genres of music ought to be encouraged. And while a given musician may not be able to adapt to a particular style, the musician should be able to provide other resources, supervise such offerings, and determine their quality and fitness for a given church in consultation with the pastor. In many cases, music is the key to reaching persons of different races, cultures, languages, ages, and backgrounds. People come with a variety of needs, traditions, gifts, and so on. The music of worship should affirm that diversity so as to be inclusive in our congregational singing and instrumental music.

Most communities include people of different races and cultures; so should the church of Jesus Christ! There are ample resources available in many forms from Asian, Hispanic, African American, and Native American Christians. I would want the cooperation of the musician. If not familiar, then get exposed. As a Wesleyan, I quote the founder, John Wesley: "... the world is my parish." It would be interesting to see what his brother, Charles, would be writing and singing these days.

5. I would hope that, along with the pastor, the musician would participate regularly in continuing education. In my denomination, it is required of pastors. I would want the musician to see this as a requirement as well. Many well-taught seminars, conferences, workshops, retreats, short-term seminary and university courses, and other opportunities are offered for church musicians. I would expect the musician to avail himself or herself of these opportunities with the local church footing the bill. Many professional organizations also provide ample opportunity for exposure to and learning of new music, music practices, new arrangements, and new ways of doing church music. While I have a serious aversion to much of the "Seven-Eleven" gospel and praise songs (seven words repeated eleven times), I cannot deny their role so often played in "folk worship" and now even in many of our mainline churches. Maybe some of our church musicians can be challenged to add some substance and some social justice content to such a genre, and then I won't mind the drums, the synthesizers, the maracas, the guitars, and the rest. After all, the Psalmist did say: "Praise the Lord with trumpet, loud cymbals, stringed instruments and organs. Let everything that has breath, praise the Lord." [Psalm 150:3-6, paraphrased]

Well, these are my reflections on what I would want my musician to know. But what I have not said, and must add *as most important*: I would want my church musician to know that his or her call to ministry is important to me and that I take calling seriously. In our joint effort to please God, we both must "study to show ourselves approved unto God, a worker that needs not be ashamed...." [2 Peter 2:15]

Adam M. L. Tice
Mennonite pastor and hymn writer
Goshen, Indiana

It may be a little self-serving for me to say as a pastor/musician, but I would like both musicians and clergy to work towards dismantling the clergy-musician dichotomy. Of course, all of us wish that clergy would all receive some level of musical training, but the reverse should be true as well. Musicians pursuing work in the church should regard themselves as pastors, because leading music for the liturgy, directing a choir, and playing guitar or organ are pastoral acts. Musicians touch on the deepest spiritual needs of congregations; to take that on with anything less than a pastoral perspective would be irresponsible. Sacred musicians do nothing less than lead people into an awareness of God's presence. They should be as prepared for that as any pastor.

Lucy Lind Hogan
Episcopal priest
Hugh Latimer Elderdice Professor of Preaching and Worship
Wesley Theological Seminary, Washington, D.C.

As a clergy person I would want them to know how important and crucial they are to the worship experience. I would also want them to know that I consider them more in a ministerial than artistic role.

I am afraid that too many church musicians come to their position in a congregation as artists and they think about what they are doing, whether it is as organist, pianist, member of a praise band, or choir director, as a performance. It is not a performance—it is part of the liturgy the same way that those reading scripture or prayers are not actors performing a play. I appreciate the way that the cantor in a synagogue is understood to be a part of the ministerial staff. I wish that our churches could adopt that approach.

Communication, negotiation, understanding, encouragement are all essential to the clergy/musician team. The musician brings talents and gifts to the planning of worship. Clergy need to listen to them and make use of their knowledge. Likewise, musicians need to listen to clergy who hope that service music, i.e., hymns, anthems, preludes, will be a theological whole. I once served at a church where the organist/choir director thought nothing of ignoring hymns that I had chosen because I believed that they complemented and amplified the theme/message of my sermon. However, I, as a clergy person, also need to listen to the music director who explains that a hymn will be too difficult for the congregation or that they do not know it.

The concept of a worship team: clergy, musicians, church educators, the visual technology group, lay readers, worship leaders, is becoming more and more important. The more people involved in planning the more chance we have of having true liturgy—the work of the people, all the people. The more people involved in planning worship, the more important it is to give plenty of time for advance planning. The days of putting the service together at the last minute are long gone.

I would also want musicians to know how challenging it is to write a sermon; to decide what to say to this group of people at this time. I would therefore ask for a little understanding and flexibility. All too often I start a sermon in one direction only to have the Holy Spirit send it off in an entirely different direction. (Wait a minute, didn't Jesus mention something about the Spirit blowing where it wills?) I might ask for a different sermon hymn at the last minute. Could that happen?

It is important for musicians to think about the theology of the music (both in word and melody). Not all music is theologically appropriate. As clergy, we are happy to sit down and explore the upcoming scripture texts, sermon, and the theological theme that is being developed.

Carol Cook Moore
United Methodist minister
Assistant Professor of Worship and Preaching
Wesley Theological Seminary, Washington, D.C.

My first memories of church are of music. The experience of being a cherub in the children's choir for the Christmas pageant began the journey of knowing a place of belonging and deep joy when the task was to listen, learn, follow, and sing! We clergy and musicians come at this partnership from our lenses of experience. Because my formative years in the church were shaped primarily by my beloved choir director, John Yarrington (Director of Music Ministry at McFarlin United Methodist Church at that time) and MUMC bell choir director Randy Hengst, I am at home in sharing the task of shaping worship. The choosing of music can be solely the musician's responsibility. Yet, how much richer our partnership in ministry and the flow of worship has been when we can share this together. Likewise, the task of crafting the worship order and content can be left to me, the pastor. Yet, how much deeper are the hues of the colors woven through this tapestry when I listen to my colleagues in music. To share in worship design requires three things: mutual respect for the expertise each of us brings to the table, clarity of responsibilities, and an openness to consider where the Holy Spirit may be nudging each of us and the congregation we are in ministry with.

Thus, what I want the musician I partner with to know:

I respect your talent and skill and training and I ask that you respect mine. The dynamic worship that is required in the church today requires of us an ability to re-inscribe the traditions of faith in a new way. The day of "you do your job and I do mine" because the slots for our contributions remain the same is ending. Vital worship requires a well woven tapestry. Therefore, I not only bring a skill set of theology and liturgy, I also need to be sharpening my skills. I ask that you would do the same. Working together allows us to learn from one another. We need to spend time together that is not just "get the bulletin done" time. We need to pray together, ponder scripture together, sing together.

In the United Methodist Church, the *Book of Discipline* states that the minister in charge is in charge of worship. It does not say that this minister is to do it all or to delegate it all. The reality is that each clergy has a way of carrying out this responsibility. When I become stubborn, it is not because I want to exert my power. It is because there is a deep theological focus or liturgical principle I am holding fast to. I need to tell you what that is and I need you to trust that if my determination falls short, I will take full responsibility. Sometimes the weight of the buck-stopping carries great apprehension. Mutual respect cultivates trust. I need to be able to trust that you will carry your weight in preparation for and leading in worship. Likewise, you need to be able to do the same.

Finally, this is not our project. This is a venture with the Triune God, week in and week out. We need to be prayerful for one another as each of us is working on a prayer, witness, confession and invitation, in song and word. We also need to listen to the congregation, even though this means enduring squeaky wheels and broken records. We also need to listen to the world outside of our congregational life, the community in our immediate context, and the big, wide world. I am not suggesting that we react to every criticism or trend. It is in prayerful listening that we may just discover something we have missed.

Cheryl Tatham
Disciples of Christ minister
North Chevy Chase Christian Church, Chevy Chase, Maryland

As a pastor in the Christian Church (Disciples of Christ) and a vocalist, I believe the music of the church speaks its theology far more profoundly than any sermon one can preach.

Coming from the free-will tradition, Disciples' liturgy is fairly free form and is not mandated by any specific formulation. That opens up to us the opportunity to structure our services of worship with a variety of elements, many of which involve music in a variety of forms. Our church musicians bring to worship their preferences in music in the repertoire he or she has mastered and enjoys. Their particular repertoire enhances the worship in its beauty and quality, but should also be in service to the congregation as a means and vehicle for opening the window to those "thin places" in worship—those moments when we experience, mistily through the veil, the presence of the Holy Other.

We Disciples received a rich heritage from our Presbyterian and Baptist roots, and also from the folk music brought to us through that Irish/Scottish heritage. This was further enhanced by the folk music of the people of Kentucky, especially in Bourbon County, Kentucky, at Cane Ridge in the early 1800's as our founders began the revivals that would set the stage for the Disciples' movement. The heritage of the spiritual in Disciples' congregations came not only from the slaves of Disciples' masters who brought them to the white congregations, but also from those freed black Disciples in their own black congregations in Midway and Logan County, Kentucky, and Morrow County, Ohio.

In today's twenty-first century church, Disciples congregations, like so many other congregations, continue to be challenged to use music that is true to our theological understandings, but also to use music that, like the spiritual, speaks to the heart of the worshiper as well. Whether instrumental or vocal, music is essential to the life of the church and its worshipers, and should be nurtured and taught to our children and our teens and our adults so that at those moments when simple words fail us, the music of our hearts will speak for us.

Reformed theologian Karl Barth, in his *Church Dogmatics*, reminds us:

> The Christian Church sings. It is not a choral society. Its singing is not a concert. But from inner, material necessity it sings. Singing is the highest form of human expression.... The praise of God which finds

> its concrete culmination in the singing of the community is one of the indispensable forms of the ministry of the church.[22]

The church cannot be the church without music. The Psalmist tells us that "even the meadow and the valley shout for joy and sing." (Psalm 65:13). How can God's people do any less? While striving to do well whatever we do musically and planning appropriately for liturgical seasons, special events, or structured liturgy, I believe that God's song (much like God's Spirit!) will burst forth from the human throat spontaneously to express the human condition and to seek out God. Whether heard in the spirituals of the slaves or in Beethoven's *Missa solemnis*, the human voice lifts toward the heavens in the throes of oppression or praise. The music of the church should seek to understand the human condition, how God is present to it, and offer voice and instrument to give praise and thanksgiving as often as we can.

Matthew Smith
Senior Pastor
St. Thomas United Methodist Church, Haymarket, Virginia

The body of Christ depends upon dedicated servants who give joyfully of their time, energy, and talents to fulfill the mission of making disciples. My hope is that anyone who is part of the ministerial team would remain committed to that purpose within and outside of their official responsibilities. Particularly in the context of corporate worship, that involves offering a sincere and powerful message of grace and hope in lyric and sound, assisting the parishioners in drawing near and praising God musically, and presenting Christ at the cost of themselves. I know that I depend upon the prayerfulness of my church musicians to help me worship and to present a message that is supported by the music. Like a pastor, they must also draw close to Christ in prayer and personal devotion, possess maturity, offer grace, have a heart for the lost, and labor to remain relevant through constant learning.

J. Philip Wogaman
Senior Minister emeritus, Foundry United Methodist Church
Professor Emeritus of Christian Ethics, Wesley Theological Seminary, Washington, D.C.

So what do I want musicians to know? First off, of course, to be pretty good at their craft (organ or piano, choral directing) so that the end product, Sunday after Sunday, contributes significantly to the tone of worship. As a United Methodist, I'd want the musician to be familiar with Methodist hymnody in order to help in the selection of appropriate hymns and to be familiar with choral and instrumental literature. As a part of a ministerial team, I'd want the music director to be collegial and to share in pastoral responsibility. In my experience, every member of a ministerial staff (in a multi-staff church) has a certain "circle" of people for whom she/he is, in effect, a pastor. That can't be too tightly defined; it's just a reality. I would expect real institutional loyalty, the capacity to receive and maintain confidences, without conveying an impression of secretiveness. I'd want the person to feel free to voice criticism directly, but not to undermine my ministry in any way.

Lovett H. Weems, Jr.
Distinguished Professor of Church Leadership
Director, G. Douglass Lewis Center for Church Leadership
Wesley Theological Seminary, Washington D.C.

1. Understand that music exists to serve the mission of worship, just as worship exists to serve the mission of the church.
2. Understand and take account of the distinctive context of the congregation and community.
3. Understand that the first role of a choir is to enhance congregational singing.
4. Take into account both theological and pastoral considerations in selecting music.
5. View success as when music connects people with the love of God in powerful ways.

Gretchen Hulse
United Methodist minister
Pastor, Veterans Administration, Pittsburgh, Pennsylvania

It sure helps if the person who is responsible for the musical component of a worship service is as passionate about music, as flexible, and as concerned about how it all fits together. I've experienced worship in numerous places. I've attended services in a wide variety of denominational styles, in a wide variety of sacred and not-so-sacred spaces. The thing that made—or killed—the worship experience was the music. If the music was on, the worship experience was just that, a worshipful experience. If the music was off, you could feel the mood of the people gathered there was not in a mode of worship.

I do my best to help lead people into a state of being open to the Spirit of God for at least an hour a week. The sad reality is that this hour is the most interaction some of my congregants will have with even the idea of worshiping God. And the truth is that most American congregations are the same way. Not all pastors want to admit that. But people aren't drawn into a healthy relationship with the Divine because of the hour, the space, or even the preacher. They are drawn into those relationships because they feel God. They experience God in the physical and spiritual. The preacher challenges them to go deeper in that relationship, but the music draws them in. I can't do it all. No one can. Nor should we. There were always musicians to lead the people into the experience of the Divine when they gathered (there are tons of references through the Old Testament). That's not just a coincidence.

We, the worship team, including the pastor, are present to help create an experience that is conducive to drawing people closer into the presence of God. We have to be the best we can be at what we do. We have to be passionate about sharing this experience of worshiping God. We have to want to see lives transformed and believe that it can begin in this hour. We have to be on the same page. It helps if we plan worship together. It helps if we, the pastors, know that the musicians are as committed to seeing lives changed as they are to giving the "best performance of their life." I've met some pastors who feel they are just there to perform or do their "job." But that's the wrong attitude. It goes the same way for the musician. That's not why we're doing what it is we believe we're called to do. I guess that's at the core of it: Do you do what you do as a musician because it's a paycheck you're seeking? or do you help usher people into the presence of God through music because that's what God has called you to do? Answering those questions honestly will make all the difference.

I'm not called to perform. I'm called to help draw people into a deeper relationship with their Creator. The moment it becomes a performance for me, I will quit. God called me for much more than mediocrity. God called me to be faithful to who I am created to be. God called me to give my best. And God can help me do what I am to do when I am honest and sincere about my talents and gifts.

Dave Hunter
Unitarian Universalist minister (retired)
Berwyn, Pennsylvania

If music is important, then musicians are important.... Ours is a small congregation, and they think of themselves as having very restricted financial resources.... But what if we could afford the best?

My ideal church musician would be an excellent musician who knows how to accompany the congregation on hymns, how to fill dead time or provide transitions, how to lead singing, how to teach hymns to the congregation, how to take the choir to musical places they had never been before, an excellent sight reader on piano or organ. He or she would be a people person, attracting people to the congregation and to the choir and inspiring their commitment, able to work with children and youth as well as with adults. He or she would help choir members become better singers. He or she would realize that the choir is more than about music, that it forms a valuable community within the congregation, and that it is a training ground for future leaders (it's where I got my start). He or she would be able to find music supportive of the theme but would also be able to play music that the congregation would find satisfying or that would stretch their musical boundaries. He or she would be politically astute, knowing how to survive church politics, committed to the whole ministry of the church and not just to the music program. He or she would not necessarily be a Unitarian Universalist, but would at least be sufficiently sympathetic to be supportive of the denomination, to be able to articulate some of the basics, and not to undercut it.

Lewis A. Parks
United Methodist minister
Professor of Theology, Ministry, and Congregational Development
Wesley Theological Seminary, Washington D.C.

1. I want musicians to appreciate the theological heritage in which the congregation and I are nurtured. Attention to that heritage regardless of the musical style is crucial. In my situation I am talking about Charles Wesley first and foremost. For a Lutheran I can image Luther and Paul Gerhardt. For Presbyterians...

2. I want them to share my ache to recover the corporate voice of the congregation! I don't want them to be part of the problem, i.e., an organist or a praise band that beats the congregation into passiveness. I want them to help recover four-part congregational singing as an expression of the congregation's vitality and attraction.

3. I want to work with them and the personnel committee of the congregation so their paid position allows as much focus as possible. I am concerned that most musicians are stringing together a score of part-time positions. If my congregation has the resources, I want to structure a decent full-time job with benefits for the lead musician. There needs to be enough security and play time to be truly creative.

4. I want them to be looking for, name, and bring forth the musical gifts of the congregation.

5. And, of course, I want them to be able to work as a contributing member of a worship team.

Kerry Mueller
Unitarian Universalist minister (retired)
Berwyn, Pennsylvania

1. Music that engages the hearts of the congregation is connected in some way to the themes of the sermon and the whole worship service and helps the congregation to sing the hymns and feel connected. Performance of music that might be beyond the ability of the congregation may be presented in other ways. Just recently, for a sermon on imperfection, I asked the music director to sing Leonard Cohen's *Anthem*, which features the line "There is a crack in everything; it's how the light gets in." She brought her adolescent son in to help and really brought down the house, setting the congregation to hear the sermon with their hearts as well as their minds.

2. The choir should be a locus of pastoral care, where people have a community of connection. This is more important to me than musical excellence, though I would like to have enough money to pay a full-time music director so that we could have at least one specialty choir for musical stretching.

3. Educate me musically, as well as the congregation and the choir.

4. Have an understanding of how churches work, so that together we can help the congregation to thrive.

5. In addition to musical excellence, this all requires imagination and tact, flexibility and personal integrity. Ministry is a difficult business. It will often break your heart. Music or religious education or pulpit, it's a constant challenge.

Walter D. (Jack) Turner
Baptist minister (retired)
Arlington, Virginia

1. Church musicians are trusted, appreciated, wanted, and are vital to modern life.

2. Choirs and other musicians are indispensable. They contribute audibly and visibly. They literally lift up our eyes (vision).

3. We enjoy their sound because we are listening to them sing to God in our behalf.

4. Musicians enable the congregation to honor, praise, give thanks, make petitions, and rejoice in God with reverence and beauty in a robust expression of worthship.

5. Musicians influence our theology. The words and emotions of music are much more powerful than prose (oratory). Music opens our ears and minds to ideas, images, feelings, convictions, righteousness, and intentions.

6. Music unlocks hidden, unexpressed, unformed, misshapen grayness into solid concepts of shame, joy, blessedness, lovingness, power, weakness, brokenness, and gladness. Healing can happen. Power can be used for good.

7. Music prepares us to appreciate silence, to welcome mystery, to be as a creature in a community by will and desire.

8 Music in church should be well prepared and presented not as entertainment, which can be distracting, but to turn us to God and the spiritual work we came to accomplish.

9. Like preachers, musicians should not call attention to themselves, thereby diverting the mind of worshipers. (A seminary classmate once left the choir loft after his solo. He ran across the street for a bag of doughnuts to eat behind the choir-draped railing during the sermon. In his hurry to return to his place, he chose the wrong door to the choir and came out on the pulpit platform down on all fours with a bag of goodies hanging from his teeth. About six feet on to the platform, he looked out at a startled congregation and pointing children. Like a well-trained dog, he backed up, still on hands and knees, and vanished out the doorway by which he entered.) Good manners are important for everyone, including musicians.

Jeffrey Haggray
Senior Pastor
First Baptist Church of the City of Washington, D.C.

It is my desire that we develop a close rapport as colleagues who are concerned for each other's mutual well-being and overall best health as co-laborers with Christ. I want us to pray together and take lunch together from time to time, and get to know each other deeply. Then it will follow that he/she will come to know and appreciate my vision and heart's desires for the church and its worship, and I will come to know and appreciate his/her heart's desires for the church and its worship. Thus, a strong professional and personal relationship based on mutual appreciation is the best foundation for serving God together. The rest will take care of itself, in my humble view.

Scott S. Ickert
Senior Pastor
Resurrection Evangelical Lutheran Church, Arlington, Virginia

Musicians and clergy must work hand-in-hand in planning and executing worship. They must work as a team. What is important in that relationship is not the individuals themselves, or their peculiar predilections and personal preferences, but the joint ministry, in which they share and are jointly engaged. Musicians are just as much theologians as are the clergy then; their calling is, if not the same, then very similar. Musicians are to apply their talents and skills, natural and acquired, to the proclamation of the gospel. There is no other reason why one should be a church musician.

Since liturgical music, including the church's hymns, conveys a message, both in form as well as in content, it is the message that should be the common concern of clergy and musician. Not only should the clergy be concerned that a particular Sunday's or feast day's texts are supported, complemented, and powerfully conveyed by the music, so should musicians be concerned that the music they select, lead and preform be faithfully articulated through scripture, sermon, sacrament, and prayer. Both clergy and musicians have a common responsibility to pass on the tradition as faithfully, artfully, and as articulately as they know how, individually, but particularly together.

When personality issues or conflicts, or even matters of taste, get in the way of this common task, then the mission and integrity of the church will suffer.

Diedra Kriewald
United Methodist minister
Professor Emerita of Teaching and Formation, Wesley Theological Seminary, Washington, D.C.

Besides knowledge of the Psalter, choral and instrumental literature, and a willingness to consider a diversity of musical styles and perspectives, in my opinion, there are three non-musical essentials:

First, being a church musician calls not just for a knowledge of the church calendar, but a musical life "lived in" the seasonal rhythms of sacred time. An enthusiasm for the calendar can be transmitted to choirs and the worshiping assembly, and be a helpful guide for discussion with the pastors.

Second, living within the structures of the church calendar should mean a commitment to the lectionary readings in the three-year cycle. The choirs are primary places of teaching and learning, and the texts for the day should be high on the list for discussion.

Third, the musician(s) should themselves study the scriptures for the worship service (whether lectionary or not), should learn how faithfully to exegete the texts, and be able to discuss the texts intelligently with the preacher and with the choirs.

Cindy Schneider
Minister for Congregational Care
Christ United Methodist Church, Bethel Park, Pennsylvania

As a second-career clergy, I had the blessing of growing up in my home church which always had a wonderful music program. Because of that background, I strive for quality and diversity in music worship. Therefore, as I worked, from the clergy perspective, and explored the talent of the church, I became aware that many of the smaller churches do not have the talent or resources that I was blessed to experience. When I came back to Pennsylvania from Washington, DC, I was appointed to a three-point charge. Two of the three churches had talented organists, and one of the churches had a young man who led the music, but there were no choirs.

Eventually, I realized that there was the potential for a more effective music program. There were people within the congregation who had the desire and ability to improve the weekly worship service. Fortunately, I was blessed with knowing how to work with these people to make our worship service more beautiful. It was a most rewarding challenge.

We, as clergy, have to be sensitive to the capabilities present, and must have the desire to work with those involved with the music ministry. We need to be aware of what they already know musically, or are able to learn. I learned from my studies at Wesley Seminary the importance of working out the hymns, sermon, and prayers for the service well in advance, so that those involved will know what to expect, and will be able to plan and have the time to practice so that worship will be a rewarding experience.

I find it enjoyable working with those who are involved in making the service creative and meaningful, so that those who are present will feel the Spirit through word and music. People will remember the music better if it complements the message. As the prayers, scripture, message, and music flow together, the message of the day is reiterated throughout the service. It's the music, however, that will help the congregation take that message with them when they leave the service. I believe that music is a truly beautiful art form, which enhances the experience of any type of worship. On numerous occasions, the hymns have been so poignant that I have encouraged the congregation to "listen" to what they are singing because it is either a prayer, or a reiteration of the scriptures and the message of the day.

My current church appointment is an entirely different dynamic. It is a large church with multiple choirs and many talented musicians. My working with our past and present organists and the Minister of Music and Worship continues to be an enormous blessing. They are great at brainstorming, assisting us with music and hymns that we might not know or think would work. They also have a wonderful gift in assisting us with music to compliment the message for the day. I have now worked with two organists and the same Minister of Music and Worship for a number of years. All are masters at writing liturgy, prayers, and formulating the day's service in order to make it meaningful and memorable.

Finally, I want to work with someone who possesses talent, love of music, and the desire to be part of a team so that we, together, can produce a service for the glory of God. It is an honor and a privilege to be part of a team striving to bring the Spirit alive through music and the spoken word.

Amy Butler
Senior Pastor
Calvary Baptist Church, Washington, D.C.

I am really fortunate to work with an excellent music staff, but this has not always been the case. In my first two years of pastoring at Calvary, four music professionals came and went for various reasons. The upheaval was frightening, disconcerting, dismaying to me. During all of this I realized: I don't even know what I want when I look for someone to be my colleague in the musical part of this work. I confess that articulating this has been a long process, largely informed by the excellent work of the colleagues I have now. So here are some things I wish all church musicians knew:

1. Worship is not a performance. That is, worship should ever and always be pointing toward God. Whenever we focus on an individual performance (musical or otherwise) we have failed at facilitating worship.

2. Music is not the only important thing in the church budget. I admire your advocacy for this part of our community life, but please know that there is always give and take in the life of a faith community. I need you to come to the table with creative ideas that do not cost way beyond our means.

3. Please don't be a diva or hire any musical staff who are. We have enough drama to deal with in our congregation.

4. Your work is the work of ministry. You do it by using very specialized means, for sure, but ultimately we are ministers of the Gospel of Jesus Christ. That should be the main expression and ultimate goal of any work you do.

5. Please remember that most people don't have the musical knowledge or appreciation that your many years of study have afforded you. Can you work hard to strike a balance between fine music and general accessibility? Those of us who do not share your talent will be forever grateful.

6. I know you have a musical specialty, just like I have a homiletic style I prefer. Please be ready to think outside the box and remember that variety is the spice of life.

7. Excellence, always. If that means singing "Jesus Loves Me" because we can do it very well, let's do it. Whatever we do, let's do it very, very well. Nothing can derail a worship service faster than really bad music.

Neil Irons
United Methodist minister
Executive Secretary, Council of Bishops, United Methodist Church
Washington, D.C.

I want musicians to have some substantial theological knowledge of what the church is about, the progressions in the liturgical year, a range of musical possibilities for the church, and be well versed in their own musical formation. As part of the church team, I hope that the musicians will participate in the planning of worship, will grow in their knowledge and skills, discuss possibilities as to the interconnection between music and the other expressions of worship, and have the interpersonal skills to be equal partners in the staff.

Notes

1. Are, 57.

2. Roberts, 28.

3. E-mail to author, August 8, 2010.

4. Lawson, 91.

5. Westermeyer, 25.

6. Kroeker, 71.

7. Hoyt L. Hickman, ed., *The Faith We Sing*, Nashville: Abingdon Press, 2000, Hymn No. 2130, stanza 4.

8. Roberts, 29.

9. Are, 53–54.

10. Ballou, *Moving Spirit*, vi.

11. Westermeyer, 11.

12. Ballou, *Moving Spirit*, 1.

13. Westermeyer, 23-24.

14. *Ibid.*, 6–7.

15. Are, 7–8.

16. Roberts, 21–22.

17. Are, 69.

18. *Ibid.*, 42.

19. [Name withheld], e-mail to author, September 26, 2011.

20. Deborah Tyree, e-mail to author, September 25, 2011.

21. Westermeyer, 29.

22. Karl Barth, *Church Dogmatics*, vol 4, ed. G. W. Bromiley and T. F. Torrance, trans. G. W. Bromiley, Edinburgh: T&T Clark, 1995, 44–60.

5

Effective Clergy: Qualities and Skills

> *For Jesus, the principle governing all relationships was love. That love was personal—person forgiving person, enemies reconciling, neighbors providing succor, parents and children finding oneness. Out of that love, people served and sacrificed.... Jesus formed circles of friends, not a hierarchical institution concerned with allocating power. Jesus saw leaders as servants, nurturing those circles, not as managers running an institution.*
>
> —Tom Ehrich, *Church Wellness*

Countless books have been written about the skills needed to be a successful pastor. While it might seem arrogant (or at least brave) for a musician to attempt to add to that body of knowledge, thanks to my time on a seminary faculty teaching hundreds of students and staying in contact with graduates, as well as a number of years serving in churches, I feel able to offer some time-tested basic qualities of a successful pastor.

Basic Assumptions

Effective clergy take seriously the role of prophet and preacher and prepare sermons with skill and passion. They are focused on worship and the ways the various parts of the service are planned and knit together. They are concerned for the congregation more than their own reputation, and they take pastoral care seriously. Their administrative skills and ability to delegate allow for an easy flow of information to and from the staff. They delight in the skills of the staff with whom they work and take pleasure in their ministry successes. They are persons of integrity in whom staff and congregation can confide with the confidence that this information will not be shared with others.

Embracing Staff Colleagues

Create an Affirming Environment

There is a saying that "the person who doesn't make mistakes is unlikely to make anything." Clergy can create an environment in which ideas are welcomed and can be discussed in a free give-and-take. This atmosphere can flourish when staff members know that no one will be unfairly criticized or publicly humiliated if an idea is not accepted or does not work out.

Make a Priority of Collegiality

The support that clergy give to ministerial colleagues is critically important to their effectiveness, and staff members often feel that they could not survive at a church without the support and encouragement of the senior pastor. There are a number of ways clergy can demonstrate collegiality. For example, make sure job descriptions are current, that there are fair and regular performance reviews, and make it a point to see that the musician's salary is adjusted when more responsibilities are added. Show appreciation for the extra effort by the musical program, especially at the most demanding times of the year such as Advent/Christmas and Holy Week/Easter, when the choirs have probably sung half a dozen services over the last three days. To the best of your ability, ensure adequate music budget, salary, and benefits for the musicians and the rest of the staff. Be available and encourage meeting with the musician not only to plan worship but also to develop a collegial relationship. Visit choir rehearsals, attend choir concerts, and support choir retreats.

Consider moving a part-time music position to full-time. While this will encourage more highly skilled musicians to apply for a vacancy, it also has proven benefits in terms of congregational vitality. "A full-time church musician who is (1) musically talented, (2) dynamic and effective as a leader, and (3) spiritually grounded will transform the congregation."[1]

Sometimes it's not easy to be a supportive colleague, as a clergy colleague shared with me in this heartfelt message:

> For me the whole issue comes to, "How do we help each other be the servants of God and of the church that we're called to be?" That's such a different question than, "How can I get what I need?" or "How can I advance despite the obstruction of my colleague?"
>
> I'm deeply aware that in the main, the church musician's authority is derivative. There are some things, maybe many, wherein the musician does not have ultimate decision-making authority, especially when the pastor views the overview and outcome of worship as her/his responsibility. What I want to ask is, "How can the pastor retain that distinctive vantage point as s/he comes to the worship planning table without being domineering or controlling?" There's no question that the senior leader has a distinctive vantage point, and it's silly for the musician to think otherwise. The point is, can the pastor use that vantage point well, and is the pastor open to the significant input that the musician and other staff members bring to worship planning?
>
> I was blessed with two long-tenured musicians who didn't question that I had a distinctive vantage point, but who insisted that they not only have a place at the table but also the freedom to speak about the overall effectiveness of Sunday morning worship.
>
> I suppose if I had a heartache with both of my musicians it was that they both criticized me for not giving them enough positive feedback (or feedback in general) while at the same time not acknowledging that, year after year, I was devoting a key amount of my energy to the institutional health issues that were not only paying their salaries, but providing them both with significant salary increases during their tenures. It was kind of like their attitude was, "Well, that's your job." Maybe, but I took some [criticism] for them when anxious finance people couldn't understand that you don't pay for hours with musicians, you pay for talent.[2]

Be Available

Schedule times with an open door. Of course, there are times when you cannot be available to staff members because you are engaged in sermon preparation, counseling, or other pastoral duties. Setting aside certain times for informal conversation with colleagues is not only affirming of their ministry, but also an invaluable way for you to stay plugged in.

Trust Your Staff

Model integrity in all you do or say and require that of others. This means, among other things, keeping confidences and respecting boundaries. Trust your staff by sharing pastoral concerns and administrative issues. Be willing to be honest and vulnerable in that sharing. Colleagues are more likely to cut you some slack if you have brought them into your world. By your example, you will encourage their deep and important sharing.

Supporting the Role of Music

Know Something about Music

We have mentioned this concept in other chapters, but it would seem wrong to omit it from this one. As Paul Westermeyer writes:

> Paradoxically, music inevitably accompanies the Christian church even when institutional supports for it are not provided. One would expect the leaders, the clergy, therefore, to have some knowledge of the church's song, even when money for music is short.... Despite some delightful exceptions, American clergy generally know little about church music, hymnody, and even worship. Part-time musicians, even ones with little training, often know more about these topics than do clergy. This statement is not so much an indictment of the clergy as it is an indictment of American seminaries.[3]

Form a Theology of Church Music

How do you view music and its role in worship? How does God speak through music to you and to your congregation? Giving it some thought will not only help you plan worship more effectively, it will also enable your work with the church musician(s). Do be sure to formulate your theology of church music *before* beginning the process of hiring a church musician.

"Some ministers see music as no more than a filler in the service of worship. They see the church musician as a hired hand employed to lead the music program. The idea that an organist or a choir director is, in fact, also in ministry and committed to the tending of souls never enters their minds."[4]

A pastor shared these thoughts about the role of music and musicians in worship:

- The congregation as a whole should be encouraged constantly to sing its faith with full voice, enjoying its old favorites while also stretching itself and learning new songs.
- If there are musically talented people within the congregation, ways need to be found to honor their gifts and use them—at least on occasion.
- A small church can be an ideal setting for students and others whose skills are not fully developed to make a contribution.
- A four-octave handbell set should not be stored in a back closet for years because there are not enough people for a full handbell choir. Same goes for other instruments around the church (e.g., tambourines and other rhythm instruments, recorders, etc.). There are ways to use them that may be appropriate at least once in a while.
- Our hymnal and the various recent supplements have lots of songs, and responses in them. The musician should learn them and try to love them all, even though there are a number of them that may never be used for congregational singing.
- The musician ideally is out ahead of the pastor and congregation in terms of enthusiasm for getting the whole congregation singing, suggesting songs and understanding the range of possibilities for special seasons.
- Selection of hymns for congregational singing should involve consultation and discussion between pastor and musician. Several months in advance, the choir director should identify for each Sunday possible hymns or songs that the congregation knows or might easily learn. During a discussion with the musician, the pastor may then suggest additions. In other words, the musician does not do all the hymn choosing, nor does the pastor, although the musician might want to respect the fact that the pastor with a theological education might be in a better position to evaluate the message of hymn texts than a musician with no theological education.
- As a pastor looking at musical possibilities for various Sundays and seasons, I would prefer to be surprised and delighted by a musician's openness to a gorgeous text or new tune—even though the congregation might have to sing it weekly for two months to get used to it—than dismayed by a musician's insistence on being limited to the congregation's existing repertoire and what its most vocal members insist are its tastes.[5]

Plan Ahead

Help the musician(s) do the job they are capable of doing by giving them information sufficiently ahead for them to locate appropriate music, practice the music themselves, and rehearse it with their ensembles.

> I value the time that it takes to prepare to lead worship. It is hard for the musician to feel a part of a team if they are not involved in or privy to the plans. Although a good musician can wing it when necessary, this should not be the norm imposed by poor planning on the part of the pastor. I value the time it takes to select, locate, and then properly rehearse music appropriate to the season or theme of worship.[6]

Generally, the relationship between a staff member and the senior clergy is important to the way the staff member feels about the church and about the job. Understand how deeply musicians care about their work. They want to please you as well as honor God and connect with the members of the congregation. And they need to know that their work matters.

Be Clear on Qualities You Seek in Musicians the Church Hires

Do you want a keyboard person, a choir director, a concert organist, a fine service player, a gospel pianist, or a praise band director? Each of these involves a different skill set. Also consider these questions: Do you want someone who cares deeply about the ministry of the church, or someone who will come in and "do the gig" competently. There are various ways to characterize potential roles. We have already referenced Paul Westermeyer's use of the term "music-grinder," as opposed to someone who cares for the full ministry of the church. William Bradley Roberts asks if the goal is to have a dedicated servant of the church or simply someone who will provide the music—a colleague or a subordinate, someone who will partner with you or someone that you can control? Those are basic decisions that should be discussed with the search committee before the position is even advertised. Roberts uses this analogy:

> I compare … the church musician to the worker you hire to paint the church steeple. You don't care how he feels about steeples, or even what he thinks about the churches underneath them. You just want to know if he can paint the steeple. Applied to the parish organist or choir director, this would be what I call the "steeple-painter church musician." How such persons feel about faith or ministry simply isn't germane, as long as they don't interfere with the larger work of the church. And perhaps for some parishes this model still works just fine. It is to the clergy of the

> other parishes, however, that I'm speaking—those clergy expect that a church musician will be a partner in ministry.[7]

In discerning what it is the church you serve might need from a musician, talk with colleagues, consult with the worship committee, access online denominational material and resources from the American Guild of Organists. There is much available to help you determine what skills are desired in a new colleague. In the interview process, share your views on the role of music in worship so the musician will have an idea of your values and whether you can work well together as a team.

Self-Care

Recognize the Temptation to Play Super Pastor

Pushing yourself to work sixty-plus hours a week does not mean that should be required of the rest of the staff. Recognize particularly demanding times of the year and do not schedule retreats or extra-long staff meetings at those times. Be sensitive to the stress of major life changes within the congregation and staff—illness, death, divorce, departures—and their effects on the congregation and staff.

It is tough to be equally good at the different roles of theologian, pastoral counselor, administrator, social advocate, supportive colleague, and family member (the latter, often in your spare time). Decisions about the ways you spend your time communicate your values to your staff and congregation. When you are not at a certain event, let people know you will be absent because there is another place where you are even more needed—it's not because you don't care. Recognize the time needed for sermon preparation, hospital visitation, pastoral counseling, or committee meetings, and decide which of these demands can be delegated to a colleague. Effective clergy, realizing they cannot do it all themselves, enlist the help of colleagues and laity.

Another dimension of the Super Pastor trap is the temptation of "a role persona," a facade that pastors sometimes adopt "as they fulfill their required roles. Wearing such a mask involves having to act in an affected manner, use appropriate tones, and say only what is expected."[8]

Remain Aware of the Ego

A healthy ego is necessary in order to do one's job. Without it you could not conduct a service, much less stand in front of your congregation and offer what you hope are words of wisdom, inspiration, and comfort. But an unchecked ego is unhealthy. Ego-driven individuals not only need their egos fed, they are jealous when others receive affirmation. "The better I did my job, the more the senior pastor hated me," one musician says. "He was jealous when a member of the congregation said how great the music had been that morning. He was jealous when someone reported to him appreciation of a pastoral response I had made to a member of the choir. He was just jealous, jealous, jealous."[9]

"Ego-driven senior pastors," writes John Setser, "consider themselves people of destiny. They expect to be obeyed."[10] Ego-driven clergy are also driven to succeed, believing themselves to be responsible for any success in the church. They feel threatened when the musician receives compliments from members of the congregation. Similarly, they feel threatened when the musician forms a spiritual community within the choir, assuming a pastoral as well as a musical role. They fail to see that "your success is my success, your failure is my failure." As Paul wrote to the Corinthians, "If one member suffers, all suffer together with it; if one member is honored, all rejoice together with it." (1 Corinthians 12:26) We are called to support each other in times of failure and times of success.

Recognize the Stress of Ambition

The drive to succeed is a major stressor. Some drive to succeed is unavoidable, because clergy are called to account by their church governing bodies. These often have a number-crunching mentality and encourage a drive to achieve increasing numbers in attendance, membership, and budget.

While there are certain denominations that are particularly concerned about the numbers game, this is a challenging time for churches in general. It is especially challenging if your church is in danger of closing; not only may you be held responsible, but the changes that need to happen in order to turn it around may be daunting. The stress that comes as a result of this pressure is addressed by church growth expert Peter Wagner, who states, "There may be exceptions, but the rule appears to be this: If a church is not growing, take a close look at … the pastor."[11]

The fallacy here, of course, is that pastors are not solely responsible for enabling or inhibiting the effectiveness of the church. Pastors who enable the ministerial team to do their work well, in a spirit of collegiality and common vision, know the good work of the team will reflect well on them. If the senior pastor tries to control everything single-handedly, then the spirit of collegiality is diminished and so is the benefit of shared ministry, including the possibility of actually achieving effective ministry.

The toll such stress can cause is alarming, and the list of results includes addiction, burnout, and departure from the ministry. Increased incidents of marital infidelity and other inappropriate behavior are also reported. "William Easum warns that today 'clergy addiction of one kind of another appears to be at an all-time high.' Senior pastors suffering from job stress can reach the point where their ministry becomes destructive. When this occurs, they become wounding agents."[12]

Unfortunately, while staff members may decide (or be forced) to leave a dysfunctional environment, the pastor remains and, unless the church takes a hard look at the pastoral responsibility in such cases, the vicious cycle just continues.

Resist the Need to Have Everyone Agree with You

This is a particularly debilitating form of dysfunction. "The defense mechanism of hostility drives damaged senior pastors to move aggressively against associates to get what they need. They are convinced that intimidation, bullying, and coercion will give them this desired result. They gain confidence and strength by controlling people and scripting outcomes."[13] There are additional complications when the senior pastor's vision is not shared by others on the staff. They may be subjected to public embarrassment, berated, or dismissed. The senior pastor's calling and vision are seen as primary, with no room for the vision of anyone else. Often, if other staff do not agree or offer an alternative that is acceptable, they are consequently labeled as "not supporting my ministry," and dismissed.

Reach Out to Friends and Colleagues outside the Congregation

A terrific concept is the recent trend by clergy to form "cohorts" or support groups. While clergy may find it difficult to share personal issues with those who might later become their supervisors, they vitally need access to emotional support and meaningful relationships outside the congregation. The ability to keep confidences and respect boundaries is essential. Both pastor and congregation will ultimately benefit.

What Musicians Want Clergy to Know

When I started teaching at Wesley Theological Seminary two decades ago, I asked a group of church musician friends for a wish list regarding their relationship with the clergy and/or the church. I ran across that list recently and found that it pretty well summarizes church musicians' wishes today.

- A relationship of trust; be treated as an equal or team member—not as an employee
- Opportunity to meet on a regular basis to discuss liturgies (past, present, and future); develop long-range dreams and plans
- Opportunity to help in hymn/service music selection process
- Just compensation (without having continually to justify salary increase request)
- Benefits: continuing education, retirement, health, book allowance, professional dues, sabbatical
- Opportunities to "play together;" develop genuine concern for each other (health, family)
- Support choirs by attending an occasional rehearsal to express appreciation—not taking choirs for granted, positive reinforcement. Choirs are a dedicated group—one of the few groups in a church that meets twice a week.
- Freedom to deal with conflict: gossip, ventilate, avoidance, agree but disagree, confront
- Adequate music budget
- Long-range planning

Not much has changed in the last twenty years. More recently, I was preparing to lecture in a corporate worship class and thought it would be interesting to ask musicians what they would want me to share with the pastors and future pastors in this class. I received a number of insightful responses at that time and offer them below, along with notes that have come from others when they learned about this book.

Emily Koons
Director of Music/Organist
St. John's Evangelical Lutheran Church, Westminster, Maryland

Church musicians love serving the Lord and the church. We love serving the people of our churches. Church musicians are interested in helping support sacred texts. We would like clergy to give theological interpretations of Bible readings so we may help choose music that supports these sacred texts. We would also like to know sermon topics in advance, and any salient points the clergy would like all who hear the readings and sermons to understand and remember.

Church musicians like planning church services with clergy, rather than simply being told what to do. Unless they are trained to be professional musicians, clergy should not assume that role. It is disrespectful. Church musicians should not assume the role of priest or minister unless trained to do so. Church musicians are professional musicians. We are trained, and usually highly trained, to do what we do.

We love our work and would like to be able to afford to continue in the honorable profession of servants of God. There is a vast difference between professionals of any occupation and volunteers, and expectations for job performance by professionals are higher. Job performance is also affected by instruments and musical talent available for the job.

Church musicians would like a working relationship with mutual respect among all vestry (or senior management volunteers), staff, and clergy at a church. Church musicians want to continue to perform music of integrity to honor the word of God.

Church musicians would like to work together with clergy toward the goal of bringing people to God. Wonderful things happen in worship and in churches when all work together.

The AGO motto—*Soli Deo gloria*—is our professional creed.

Many church musicians have left the church permanently due to a number of unfortunate and often disrespectful situations. Trust in the clergy by both staff and congregation has seriously eroded in recent years. Unfortunately, clergy have the power to fire church musicians, even after years of faithful musical service to a church, and this has happened to several of my most talented organist colleagues. It would be wonderful to see an improvement in the relationship between clergy and musicians, and to see a regained, earned trust in those who are heads of churches.

Kenneth Lowenberg
Minister of Music emeritus
Chevy Chase Presbyterian Church, Chevy Chase, Maryland

Trust your professional musician and his/her musical knowledge, taste, and wisdom. Do not micro-manage him/her. Your professional musician has spent a small fortune and untold hours of classes, lessons, workshops, and specialized training in everything related to church music. That is the person to whom you must turn for making informed decisions about what music is appropriate for your congregation. Perhaps your colleague at a neighboring church has a larger membership than you do, so naturally you want to do whatever it takes to get a larger membership yourself. But do not assume that dumping your music program and trying to emulate them is the answer. Far too many clergy are swayed by the latest passing trends or fashions in music, and they prevail upon their professional musicians to produce music that is far below the capacity and taste level of the congregation, all in the name of "trying to draw in new members" or "trying to be more relevant to the community." Don't be too quick to throw out the baby with the bathwater and try to change the musical tastes of your congregation from good quality music that has stood the test of time in favor of the latest ditties, which, like the lilies of the field, soon wither and pass away.

Michael Wu
Director of Music
Faith United Methodist Church, Rockville, Maryland

The sharing of hymn selections and planning in advance (read: at least one month) allows musicians greater opportunity to plan choral music and special music selections that are themed with the pastor's intent for specific worship services.

For clergy who eschew or work in denominations not employing the lectionary, planning ahead allows musicians, especially those charged with teaching volunteer choristers, soloists, bell ringers, or instrumentalists, to select repertoire that matches principal themes to be utilized by the preacher.

Speaking for myself, answering to a senior pastor or rector or clearly defined entity on a consistent basis makes working conditions predictable and operate smoothly. In circumstances where laity and guest speakers alter the course of worship themes and planning, respect for an incumbent musician as the resource for that planning, as opposed to a musician doing only what non-musicians believe will work, needs greater emphasis.

In situations where the musician is part time but the clergy are full time, there needs to be respect for the musician's time in regards to meetings and non-musical obligations. Meeting the musician on a mutually-agreed upon and predictable basis helps foster that respect and collegial work. Scheduling staff meetings and individual meetings whimsically or without regard to the musician's work schedule does not.

While the fact is that the buck stops at a clergy person's desk with regard to the overall worship experience and life of a church, the church would be rewarded if musical leadership tasks—building a choir, selecting hymns, coordinating special music or choral anthems—are done by someone with a professional view who specializes in those areas.

If there are many ways and many talents and responsibilities in God's kingdom, having musical ensembles of the church compete with Christian education rather than be incorporated as an integral part of said program does little for any church, especially in a day and age when a significant number of traditional churches are struggling to be relevant and stay large enough to afford their clergy, staff, and buildings.

The same leadership strategies that are the talk of corporate and non-church institutions work for church relations: stand behind your employees publicly; share your concerns about employee behavior or work in private. If circumstances warrant disciplinary action or severance, clearly, that would be public. But having congregation members complain about the speed of a hymn or how a director has a boring rehearsal—and many similar but not church-threatening issues—should not.

Leslie Wolf Robb
Director of Music Ministries
St. Paul's Lutheran Church and School, Pacific Beach, California

As a musician, I want the pastors with whom I work to know that I value and appreciate time we spend as a staff talking, studying scripture, praying, and having fun together. Knowing one's colleagues is invaluable in building trust, good working relationships, and a willingness to try out the other person's ideas.

I'd like pastors to be more courageous in trying new things in worship based on musicians' suggestions. Just because they haven't experienced it personally or it hasn't been done in their denomination doesn't mean it isn't valid.

Beryl Elwood
Organist
Mission del Sol Presbyterian Church, Tempe, Arizona

What do we want clergy to know? Same old, same old, I expect. Get us those hymns and sermon topics and texts way ahead—early enough to order music and prepare it. It eases stress on the planners and on the choirs and bell ringers, who then have time to learn and get comfortable with the music before they must perform it, and on organists who like to coordinate and learn voluntaries for the events and hymns of the day! Is worship like a random patchwork quilt or should it be designed to maximize its impact on the worshiper?

Thank goodness for the lectionary! When my pastor decides to abandon the lectionary for a while, I'm back to generic music, able to plan only for major feast days. Or just follow the lectionary anyway! I was once organist at another church where the pastor did not follow the lectionary, but he went to the beach for a week by himself in summer and again after the first of the year and returned each time with all his sermon topics, texts, scripture readings, and hymns for the ensuing months for us musicians! O bliss!

Our pastor is very good about choosing hymns that go with the lectionary, but probably to a fault, for all three hymns coordinate with the readings. Our young people have no opportunity to acquire a favorite hymn, for we seldom sing a hymn twice in a year! Maybe we could use general hymns for opening and closing and emphasize the sermon topic with the sermon hymn, which follows the sermon at our church. The old timers already have a repertoire of favorite hymns from churches past—let's give the youth a chance to develop favorites, too.

Deborah Hess
Assistant Organist
Vienna Seventh-day Adventist Church, Vienna, Virginia

Please plan ahead and get me the service information in advance. I know things will change from time to time. However, don't excuse your lack of planning as the Holy Spirit's leading. I had a pastor who would change things on the spur of the moment, because the Holy Spirit told him to make the change that morning. I believe my God is a God of organization and order. Do things happen at the last minute from time to time? Yes. However, it should not be a weekly occurrence.

Julie Vidrick Evans
Director of Music
Chevy Chase Presbyterian Church, Chevy Chase, Maryland

- Psalms were meant to be sung.
- Many of us actually have a lot of experience choosing hymns and putting liturgies together and welcome a collegial approach to same.
- If clergy are not bound by the lectionary, ideally, they need to advise of texts at least six months in advance.
- When any program of the church is going well, it is a good thing for the whole church and the clergy.

Name withheld

This is not directly about worship, but this is what I want clergy to know, and it is about the organist shortage. I want clergy to know that organists come from congregations before they come from music schools. If clergy are lamenting a lack of organists, they need to ask how many organists their congregation has produced lately. They need to ask what clergy and their associations are doing to support their organists in recruiting and training the next generation of organists. Does their parish have students who are taking piano lessons, who might enjoy some kind of "Possible Organists Club" with meetings and outings and mentoring? Is the organist [encouraged] to develop this or other training opportunities for youth?... Clergy often assume it is the responsibility of organists to volunteer to recruit and form the next generation of organists. But I think it is the leadership of the church that really needs to step up to the plate and institutionally support this work.

- We often plan things months in advance.
- We cannot always honor requests, like piano lounge musicians.
- It takes volunteer choirs more than a week to learn a choral work from the *Messiah*.
- We like you and really believe in what you are doing and want our ministries to support your ministries.

Notes

1. Roberts, 41.
2. [Name withheld], e-mail to author, September 25, 2011.
3. Westermeyer, 8.
4. Are, 8.
5. [Name withheld], e-mail to author, September 26, 2011.
6. Lauren Lay, e-mail to author, December 2, 2011.
7. Roberts, 20-21.
8. John K. Setser, *Broken Hearts, Shattered Trust: Workplace Abuse of Staff in the Church,* [n.p.], 2006, 24.
9. [Name withheld], e-mail to author, October 1, 2011.
10. Setser, 17.
11. *Ibid.*, 19.
12. Quoted in *Ibid.,* 27.
13. *Ibid.*, 15.

6

Two Are Better than One: Strategies for Developing a Supportive Relationship

Two are better than one, because they have a good return for their labor: If either of them falls down, one can help the other up. But pity anyone who falls and has no one to help them up. Two are better than one because they have a good return for their labor.

—*Ecclesiastes 4:9-10*

We have this testimony from the Hebrew scriptures on the value of teams, and from the New Testament we know that Jesus sent his disciples out not singly, but as teams. We have read in a previous chapter about the value of teams. So then, how is an effective clergy-musician team formed? What steps need to be taken so that the clergy and musicians begin to operate not as separate entities, but as a team?

It is really all about relationships. I envision a team where both partners make building their relationship a top priority, committed to giving and not just to getting, a relationship in which responsibility is shared and mutual support offered. This team would clarify their goals, roles, and ways to deal with conflict; they would commit to using the talents and knowledge of team members effectively, and pledge a willingness to be creative and take risks. These are among the many ingredients that it takes to form an effective team. Here are strategies for achieving that kind of relationship.

Develop an Understanding of Roles

First of all, develop a common understanding of the roles of musician and clergy. For example, the musician may be accustomed to choosing the hymns and may also have taken on other roles not customarily in a musician's portfolio or in the job description. How closely does the job description resemble what they actually do?

A new pastor may have a vision for the way the musician approaches his or her job and may want the musician to take on new responsibilities and to relinquish others. This requires a conversation: the pastor needs to know the existing practice of staffing and worship responsibilities. Then the team can agree more collegially on specific tasks, a timeline, and the person responsible in each instance. One pastor tells this tale:

> For my first Sunday in a new appointment I had sent the organist a list of hymns. I was unable to contact her during the week. When I arrived at the church, she said to me, "I didn't like your hymns so I changed them all." Thus began her three-year battle to prove that women pastors know nothing about music and hymn choices.[1]

With staff changes, musicians need to have a clear understanding of the church's staffing patterns. The senior pastor might indicate that s/he is the head of the staff and wants to run the show, even to the point of being advised ahead of time about issues or concerns that are going to be brought to staff meetings. Or, the pastor might say, "we work collegially as equals and we just want to keep each other in the loop." A third pattern could be, "we all are employees of the church and each of us reports to the head of the personnel committee." Or, maybe "just don't surprise me." Whatever the pastor's leadership style is, the primary task is getting everyone on the same page and, if changes are to be made, ensuring that the parties involved discuss and understand the changes and how they will be implemented.

When musicians and clergy begin working together, one of their first conversations should concern the relationship the clergy wants with the musician. Is it that of friend, or is it more supervisory, collegial, cheerleading, or evaluative? While it may take time to work out the most effective approach, and that may change as they learn to trust each other more fully, clarifying the relationship from the start leads to a solid foundation upon which to build a team.

Share Goals

Sharing personal, professional, and ministerial goals helps identify goals team members have in common. While there will rarely be unanimous agreement, it is valuable to know where the other stands in order to find sufficient common ground for working together.

Is there a goal of greater outreach to the homeless in the neighborhood? Or increasing worship attendance by those under the age of thirty? Is there a desire to involve more children in the church school or the bell choir? Does the congregation desperately need more space? Or is the building too large for the current program? Should ways be explored to make use of under-utilized space? Does a staff member desire more prayer and study time with colleagues? Ideally, staff members would be brought into the discussion so that the goals are not just those of the pastor, an individual staff member, or the lay leadership. Because any of these goals impacts more than one program area, the ideas and support of the entire staff will affect the success of the initiative.

Be a Team Player

Show genuine concern for all ministry areas. It is discouraging to work with individuals who think theirs is the only program in the church that really matters, and that it is all about them. As team members, we not only care about each other, we demonstrate sincere interest in all areas of ministry. (A word to musicians: reach out. Ask if you can lead singing when lunch is served for the homeless or if it would be helpful for you to set up a plan for singing in church school classes.) The church is strengthened when staff support each other's programs. Sincere interest in other ministry areas is a sure way never to be accused of not being a team player—probably the most damaging of all judgments.

> A big thing that has kept me [here] is the sense that we're all in it together, really interested in each other's ministries. I'm absolutely free to lead without [others] asking questions in my area, but there is such support there. And I'm just as interested in the youth ministry as in the adult ministry. We're just all building up each other's ministry.[2]

Work toward a Common Understanding about the Role of Music in Worship

Clergy and musicians will need to share their views of the role of music in the liturgy. How do *you* experience music as supporting and enhancing the other elements of the service? Music constitutes a large portion of a service, but it is only a part of the liturgy—and its full integration in worship, a multi-faceted art form, is vital. As one priest says, "Music attracts people here, and keeps them coming back, not just for performances, but for the liturgy."[3]

In discussing the role of music in worship, make sure to discuss your particular views on the role of the congregation and reasons many feel the congregation is the most important "choir" in the church. "The community is the choir, and the choir augments the community," says one musician.[4] So closely are the sermon and anthem connected in one church that the senior pastor "considers the anthem to be a second sermon."[5]

Another pastor puts it in these words: "While liturgy may be *valid* without music, it is *lacking* without music. Music brings a whole new dimension into the liturgical experience of the congregation that informs, inspires, lifts up, and empowers it."[6] Here are thoughts from other clergy and musicians.

> *A musician writes:* I believe that all musicians believe in music as art, but music in worship touches us at a different, deeper level. I come from a Methodist heritage where Charles Wesley wrote thousands of hymns that transmit our theology in song. I have seen newcomers and life-long members alike learn our theology not from a well-crafted sermon, but from a tune they can carry with them and hum the rest of the week. I want to teach the deep theological truths we hold dear.[7]

> *A pastor writes:* Music is eighty percent of the worship experience. Not just because we sing songs, or hear music for eighty out of one hundred percent of the time. It is music that drives the worship experience in America. It is music that inspires and encourages people when they can't or won't hear the message. It is music that acts as a connector for folks with the Divine presence. It's music that strikes a "chord" within the soul that awakens the body to act out their love and devotion to God in that hour.
>
> Let me put it another way. If the music doesn't do all those things, then it doesn't matter what else takes place in the hour-long (or more) service. You can have the best preacher in the world, but if the music doesn't draw people into the presence of the Divine, then people aren't going to be where they need to be to receive what God has to say to them through that preacher.[8]

Cross-Train

A solid clergy-musician team is best based on a certain amount of knowledge of each other's discipline. Musicians need to understand theological and liturgical language, have a basic grasp of church history and the Bible, and know what it takes to write a sermon. Clergy need to have an acquaintance with music, knowledge of sacred music repertoire, and an idea of what it takes to play with hands and feet at the same time, while simultaneously conducting with your head (or eyebrows). Both professionals need to develop an appreciation for the years it took to develop their particular skills. There is much support for the concept, "You can't make worship fit together if you haven't learned to speak a little of each other's language."[9] A pastor says:

You can't make worship fit together if you haven't learned to speak a little of each other's language.

> From my own experience, there is no substitute for pastors having at least some musical training and church musicians having some theological training. We can't send every church musician to seminary to get a master's degree in sacred music, nor is every pastor going to be able to take piano lessons or voice lessons. Some have a real appreciation for music, and some don't. Seminaries are being asked to do more and more these days, and I recognize that. But it would be so helpful for pastors to see the liturgy through the eyes of the musician and for musicians to see what they are doing in the church from a theological view and not simply as musical performance, technique, and theory.[10]

Similarly, a musician writes:

> I recall one rare experience when minister, choir director, and organist (me) completely agreed on the spiritual content of the service and made glorious music every Sunday. It is so often the opposite. Seminaries should add a course in musician appreciation![11]

There are cases, of course, where this cross-training has taken place. This can be most helpfully viewed as a gift and not as a threat. As a pastor wrote me:

> What is most important is respect and communication between the clergy and the musician(s). Many clergy do read music and some are musicians themselves; acknowledge their musical expertise (however much or little that may be!). Many musicians have seminary degrees; acknowledge their theological expertise (however much or little that may be). Ideally the musician and clergy are a team (regardless of their training in the other's discipline), working together to create worship that speaks to their particular congregation in their particular circumstances.[12]

Hold Staff Meetings

With busy part-time employees or volunteers, staff meetings are often overlooked or are set aside because of other interests and goals. It is amazing and somewhat alarming to see how many churches do not have regular staff meetings. For them it seems easier to have a quarterback calling the plays (often, the senior pastor) than it is to discuss the broader church's ministry as a group. For years in my workshops and articles, I have recommended staff meetings, and countless people have told me, sometimes years later, "You know what you said about having staff meetings? It really made a difference in our church!"

Staff meetings are designed to help team members arrive together at decisions such as (1) who is responsible for what duties, (2) what deadlines apply to which tasks, and (3) what situations drive each of us crazy. Without meetings, miscommunication can easily arise and result in easily avoidable conflict. For instance, the church secretary is working different hours and now needs bulletin information earlier than before; the young man who has been closing the building has left and someone else needs to take that responsibility; a group wants to rent the church hall but that will make it impossible for the praise team to rehearse at their usual time. Information can be communicated by e-mail, but many issues facing a church, large or small, need discussing, and that happens most effectively in person.

Scheduling these meetings at a time when everyone can attend can be a challenge when some of the staff are part time and have responsibilities at other jobs. It is worth working to find a time when at least the program staff can meet to discuss the full program of the church, to debrief on the entire ministry effort, to address problems, and especially to plan worship. If possible, include key volunteers in staff meetings at least occasionally, not only for affirmation, but also for planning purposes.

Whether clergy and musician(s) meet weekly, monthly, or even quarterly, they do need to meet to plan worship. Whether the pastor preaches from the lectionary, topically, or in a sermon series, pastor and musician need to meet. In bringing ideas to the table, it is valuable to think ahead about why an anthem, hymn, or act of worship feels right for the service. This is a wonderful opportunity for sharing and reinforcing the team process.

It may be that the greatest advantage of staff meetings is "face time," the opportunity to be together in the same room and look each other in the face as you talk. Relationships are simply harder to build and maintain without the opportunity to meet in person. These meetings may include devotions offered by staff members or discussion of a topic or a book all have read that will expand the ways you do ministry.

For longer-range planning, vision evaluation, and larger issues, a staff retreat is highly recommended. The greatest benefit is when all can go away overnight, but even a day off site can bring great rewards. A musician writes this about the importance of planning:

> It seems no one talks to anyone and the music department selects what it wants, the clergy select what they want, and when you get the bulletin on the organ bench on Thursday, you find out what the music is for Sunday! (I'm not making this up!) And if you practice prelude, postlude, and offertory three to four weeks in advance, you select without knowing what the others are going to do. It was several years before I found out they didn't want soft hymns during communion, but preferred bland "elevator-quasi new age" music instead! No one said a word.[13]

One musician summarizes team-building benefits and strategies:

> In the fifteen years I have served my current church, I have worked with five lead pastors (one of them an interim pastor). Understandably, each pastor has come with his or her own set of skills in working collaboratively. I have learned that foundational to our clergy-musician relationship must be a mutual respect for our calls and gifts for ministry. When the mutual respect has not been there, then we have essentially functioned on separate, parallel tracks. When that foundation was there, even though I found myself caught up in an admittedly love-hate relationship with the pastor, we both kept up with the dance because we knew God was at work in the other. At one point, both this pastor and I began to recognize that our relationship became strained when she was not available (either physically around or emotionally because of family or her health issues). There never seemed to be a good time to discuss the various issues as they arose. Our relationship improved significantly once that reality was recognized.
>
> The importance of accessibility has become even clearer to me in my relationship with my current lead pastor (in his sixth year at this church). In his first two to three years we got along fine on the surface, but essentially, we worked independently of each other. Then, inspired by a model picked up at a conference, we decided to try a different approach for worship planning. The pastors and I began meeting at the beginning of each week to review the worship service from the previous Sunday and to look to the Sundays ahead. (These are in addition to the regular weekly staff meetings.) The Sunday review has become an important opportunity for us to be able to discuss the ins and outs of a service in a constructive, non-threatening manner. In looking to Sundays ahead,

> we look at the scriptures (usually going with the lectionary) and select the hymns together. As we consider the possible hymns, it gives me the opportunity to say things like, "If we choose this hymn, we need to commit to singing it often enough for the congregation to get to know it." There is terrific give and take among the three of us. There are no territorial tensions. We don't always agree and we don't always even go with the majority opinion. Sometimes we trust the person who has the strongest feeling about something. It would be so easy to say we just don't have time to meet this week and return to a less integrated means for preparing worship. It makes a tremendous difference in our relationship, in my personal motivation, and in our worship when these worship-planning times are honored.
>
> It is significant to me to have experienced such a dramatic improvement in my relationship with a given pastor. We had what would probably be described as an average compatibility relationship prior to our weekly worship planning sessions. I can now say that these planning sessions have led to the strongest clergy-musician relationship I have experienced anywhere. It gives me an opportunity to provide meaningful input into the planning of worship, not just how the music will fit around what I've been given. It provides opportunities for us to interface and commiserate with each other. I find I am able (and probably more willing) to give the pastors strong support as they do me when faced with issues or personalities that might undermine our ministries.[14]

Worship Evaluation

The clergy-musician partners need to know what each values. Besides excellent, soul-stirring music and powerful preaching, do we value a beautifully constructed liturgy? Do we value flow in the service and do we care that the elements of the service connect with each other? Does it matter if the service begins on time and that it does not go longer than an hour? Is our highest aspiration having the public address system go the entire service without screeching?

There are complexities to a situation that may not be readily apparent. An example illustrating a need for clarity might be the pastor's greeting people in the narthex as they arrive for worship, making the service start late. The musician has emphasized punctuality with the choir and the choir is waiting to enter. The musician, however, may not realize that the choir's presence in the narthex is blocking those entering the sanctuary or that the choir's pre-service chatter disturbs those already in the sanctuary. The musician also may not realize the importance of a conversation the pastor is having with someone who has suffered a family loss or is in crisis and needs to share that with the clergy at that very moment. The clergy, on the other hand, may not realize the difficulty these pastoral conversations cause both the choir and musician (especially the musician, who is embarrassed at having made a big deal of having the choir in the narthex *on time*). Both parties should recognize how their differing priorities affect the worship experience. Without clear feedback from each other, neither person will know what solution will work best for all concerned.

The staff most involved in worship should regularly review the previous week's services. While logically this would happen in staff meetings, such evaluation could also be done by a worship planning team. Some churches keep a "Monday morning notebook" in which staff members make notes about the services but, to allow for perspective, are not allowed to write in it until at least Monday morning. Here they can acknowledge what went awry as well as what was particularly effective. Regardless of how the evaluation takes place, a calm and respectful approach is best, especially when there has been a crisis like the one described below, shared by a musician:

> Last Sunday we had prepared diligently for World Communion. Everything was ready. But it wasn't. What we hadn't prepared for was the unexpected. We left the choir room and climbed into the choir loft to discover electricians hanging wires all over the place. The power was out, the organ was non-functional, circuit breakers had flipped, and reset buttons had to be located. The sound technician had a major meltdown and began to cry quietly. The situation negatively triggered two choir members with early stages of dementia. They had to be calmed down and decisions had to be made on whether they stayed or left the loft. Tempers flared on about three or four fronts. It was chaos!
>
> And from the front of the church the pastor glared at me because the service wasn't going to start on time. There was no way to communicate what was happening except through crude sign language. [He apparently couldn't see the workers.]
>
> Monday morning the pastor and I sat in his office and calmly talked about not only how we could have handled the situation better, but also what we did right. And I do mean *we*. It had to be a joint evaluation. By the way, it was a very fine communion service and the congregation was inspired by what they saw and heard.[15]

Address Team Process

Is the staff a family, or a disparate group of individuals who happen to work for the same institution? How are members of a team expected to treat each other? How are they expected to communicate? Is there a protocol regarding e-mail and Facebook? All these are issues that can cause difficulties. "Triangulation" can be a particular problem in a church context. This occurs when Person A, the Complainer, has a problem with Person B but comes to you, Person C, to complain instead of dealing directly with the source of the problem (Person B). Avoid being drawn into triangulation games as the third party. Instead, direct the Complainer back to Person B or offer to have that person contact the Complainer. Do not be so pleased at having someone confide in you that you become a part of a conflict that can lead to misunderstanding and mistrust within the church staff and the whole church.

In a healthy environment, staff members agree to speak directly with each other when a problem arises—not complain to another colleague, a choir member, or a member of a church committee or the congregation. If the problem is serious and needs to be addressed, there are suggested strategies in Chapter 7.

Collaborate

This means *co-labor,* work together, on a level playing field. Each individual, whether part-time, full-time, or volunteer, is encouraged to contribute to the discussion and all ideas are warmly welcomed. An idea may not be the right one for a particular situation, but it is accepted respectfully, for what it is—*a possibility.* As one clergy colleague remarked, "The era of 'the silo' is over—it is no longer an effective strategy, if it ever really was."

A team can be quickly and easily derailed when there is confusion about who is in charge or when someone reverts to an authoritarian style. Neither the staff nor the congregation is well served by this. Yes, everyone sitting around the table knows that the most senior clergyperson is where the buck stops, but when that person operates collegially, shares responsibility, and does not pull rank, the result is a feeling of collegiality and teamwork that inspires their ministry. Collaboration allows the team to employ the skills of everyone, which is really the essence of teamwork.

Complete, Don't Compete[16]

A staff who feel in competition with each other is not productive. "A competitive spirit focuses on my ministry, while a cooperative spirit focuses on our ministry," writes Kevin Lawson in *How to Thrive in Associate Staff Ministry.* "A competitive spirit is unsettling to all involved, creating a climate of suspicion and making fellowship in ministry difficult to attain. A cooperative spirit and harmony that develops as you work together encourages longevity and satisfaction in ministry."[17]

In other words, if we "complete rather than compete," we focus on the mind-set of abundance, not of scarcity; we focus first on the organization and second on ourselves; we think "win-win" rather than "win-lose." If praise comes to one person, the amount of praise available for another is not diminished. The programs of the church, like the team members, are interdependent. If the education program attracts new children to church school, that enhances other programs too, not only because of possible new singers for the children's choir, but also because their parents might be drawn to other church programs.

Paul, in his first letter to the Corinthians, put it best, "Now there are varieties of gifts, but the same Spirit; and there are varieties of services, but the same Lord; and there are varieties of activities, but it is the same God who activates all of them in everyone." (1 Corinthians 12:4-6)

One pastor contrasts her approach to that of her colleagues: "One of the differences is that I don't see the musicians as being my adversaries. I have known pastors who did feel that way. And I've known musicians who, through experience, have felt that pastors were their adversaries and that you always had to 'fight over turf.' "[18]

"A rising tide floats all boats"—"what is good for you is good for me" is the aspirational concept here. This principal is affirmed by one clergyman, who is "as pleased to hear compliments about the music as he might be to hear compliments on a sermon. He does not distinguish between the two. The goal is to provide the people a way to worship authentically."[19]

While competitive feelings may arise, suppressing them is not the answer. When one has worked hard with little affirmation, share those feelings with the pastor. When one's program appears to have been given short shrift in favor of one that seems less critical, bring that to the attention of the appropriate people.

Respect Each Other

Mutual respect is essential in a relationship that is as close as that of clergy and musicians. Charlotte Kroeker notes that successful teams frequently use the words "respect" and "colleague."

> Dialogue, a genuine conversation, results in good communication between clergy and musician even when neither has substantial training in the other's field, provided they share an appreciation of and respect for one another. This exchange of ideas allows them to use each other's gifts effectively. Most of our respondents work in consultation with one another and achieve remarkable results. Those interviewed report how much they learn from the other person when working in dialogue and how much they appreciate working together. Over time, their vocabulary and knowledge of the other field grows.... Though the denomination's polity may establish the clergy member as the head of the team, as a practical matter these clergy/musician teams work as partners. Each brings different but equally important expertise to a common task.[20]

A musician writes of a mutually respectful relationship with his pastor:

> I have a wonderful relationship with my pastor. It is very good when the senior minister acknowledges and appreciates the fact that the minister of music is trained and, as a saved servant of the Lord, is also anointed to handle the task of supervising the music ministry. He allows me to walk in my authority as the minister of music, and I remember on one occasion his saying to me that I was the expert in my field and therefore he accepted my judgment. His door is always open (as it should be), and I feel like I can come talk with him at any time. Although we do not have a regular conference schedule, I simply catch him when I can for anything I need. His gracious spirit helps us to bond and have a fruitful and loving relationship!
>
> In contrast, at another church where I was the minister of music, I felt more like a puppet. The minister would change my hymns from time to time after I had carefully and prayerfully chosen them, especially mindful of the liturgical year. He was seldom around when I needed to talk to him, so in making an appointment with him, I felt like a stepchild. He was not always up front with me, and therefore things would get back to me that he was not pleased with when all he had to do was talk with me. I would have been receptive, prayerful, and open-minded. I remember on one occasion when I made a decision concerning the very fine pipe organ because some work was being done in the sanctuary. I was told (not by the pastor, actually by the finance officer) that she was making it explicitly clear that I was not to make any decisions concerning the organ in the

> future. I thought to myself, "Wow, that is really usurping the authority of the minister of music." I felt like I was not being allowed to do the job that I was hired to do, and I also did not feel that I had the full support of the senior pastor.[21]

The Rev. John Thornburg, clergyman and musician, shares these thoughts:

> The one quality that has the potential for making the pastor-musician relationship the most intense and wonderful is respecting and admiring each others' spirituality.... For myself, I want to know that we're on the journey together; that we're trying to get to the core of what God is doing through worship and music of the church. I know I needed to affirm my musicians for their talent and professionalism, but why are we working together in a church if not so God can use us for God's extraordinary purposes?[22]

Develop Trust

Teamwork is built on trust, which means each member of the team is trustworthy, trusts others, and is committed not to building empires, but to building up the other. "The big issue," as one clergyman says, "is trust, which is earned with time. My observation is that it takes five years in place for this to be optimal—a long five years."[23] A corporate executive explains in the book *Teamwork: What Must Go Right/What Can Go Wrong:* "Trust is something that is a must. Trust is so fundamental in terms of what a team has to value. It's never absent very long on any team. It can't be."[24] Trust is not only the foundation of a team; the absence of trust is one of the roots of team dysfunction. And one of the requirements of close effective working relationships and true collaboration is trust.

There are many ways to develop the capacity for trust in a team. A few of the most significant ones are these:

- Practice sharing honestly and openly with colleagues.
- Telling the truth at all times—even when it is inconvenient or uncomfortable or casts you in a bad light. Lies are like land mines: every time a lie is told and uncovered, there will forever be doubt about anything you say or do ("Is that really true *this* time?").
- Keeping your word—doing what you promise to do, when you said you would do it—enables people to know that they can rely on you.

- Maintaining confidence when a member of the congregation or choir has shared something with you that you do not have permission to pass on. Breaking a confidence is similar to telling a lie in that people may never again feel they can trust you. It takes a long time to build trust; it takes only a nanosecond to destroy it. Once trust has been broken, it is practically impossible to restore. The church preaches forgiveness and reconciliation; nevertheless, it takes a very long time to re-forge bonds that have been broken. Sometimes that never happens.

Notes

1. Dawn Robbins, e-mail to author, September 28, 2011.
2. Lawson, 33.
3. Kroeker, 24.
4. *Ibid.,* 50.
5. *Ibid.,* 108.
6. *Ibid.,* 105.
7. Greg Gray, e-mail to author, December 2, 2011.
8. Gretchen Hulse, e-mail to author, August 22, 2010.
9. Kroeker, 171.
10. *Ibid.*
11. Dorothy Young Reiss, e-mail to author, October 2, 2011.
12. Martha Daniels, e-mail to author, October 11, 2011.
13. Dorothy Young Reiss, e-mail to author, October 2, 2011.
14. Kathy Ritchie Toole, e-mail to author, September 26, 2011.
15. John David Horman, e-mail to author, October 4, 2011.
16. Maxwell, *Teamwork 101*, 102.
17. Lawson, 32.
18. Kroeker, 170.
19. *Ibid.*, 130.
20. *Ibid.,* 185-186.
21. Everett Williams, e-mail to author, October 10, 2011.
22. John Thornburg, e-mail to author, September 25, 2011.
23. Kroeker, 152.
24. Larson and LaFasto, 94 .

7
Dealing with Conflict

When it comes to approaching problems, you really have only four choices: flee them, fight them, forget them, or face them.

—John C. Maxwell, *17 Essential Qualities*

Avoid Harmful Conflict

The inability to deal with conflict is one of the five reasons for a dysfunctional team, according to Lencioni. Clergy and musicians both tend to be conflict-avoiders and people-pleasers. It is no surprise, then, that they don't deal well with conflict, even when it is unavoidable.

"Unresolved conflict is one of the major contributors to [associate staff] members leaving their positions," says Kevin Lawson, who offers two requirements for conflict resolution: first, a non-defensive spirit of humility willing to listen to criticism and second, respect for those with whom you find yourself in conflict and a commitment to work together as a team.[1]

Not all conflict is bad. This chapter deals not with conflict in general, but with harmful conflict. The first strategy to avoiding harmful conflict is to build a healthy relationship, and there are multiple suggestions earlier in the book for ways to do so. But if conflict arises, which threatens to become serious, there are important things you can do to minimize its harmful outcomes.

Here is wisdom that comes out of the experience of a church musician and leadership authority, Hugh Ballou:

> We have all been a part of a committee, staff, or board where unnecessary conflict arises which might make us feel uncomfortable. Some people thrive on creating energy that is directed at them.... It is therefore important to observe the conflict and attempt to control [oneself] as the process unfolds. We can't control the actions of others; however, we can control ourselves. If we are the leader, we can control process as well.
>
> Conflict happens. That's it. Conflict is energy. Conflict is creativity. Conflict lets the leader know that people are engaged. Conflict does not have to be destructive.[2]

Three Principal Causes of Conflict

Lack of Clarity

Lack of clarity may well be the greatest source of conflict among members of a church staff. This isn't about who's the boss, because the official documents of most denominations make that quite clear. It is about the division of labor, the way decisions are made, and the manner in which different views are negotiated. Conflict is more easily managed when expectations are clear. Key questions include what needs to be done, in what manner, by when, by whom, and with whom. Everyone is served when these expectations are clear.

Lack of clarity may well be the greatest source of conflict among members of a church staff.

Musicians: be assertive about your job description. You need to be told clearly what is expected of you; what latitude you have; what you can expect in order to do your job well (in terms of support, information, budget, resources); how raises are determined (cost-of-living across the board, or merit-based). When expectations are not made clear, the conflict between staff members can loom large.

These responsibilities should be in writing, specifically, a letter of agreement or a contract and an up-to-date job description. Conflict may still arise, but at least this will provide a basis for discussion if there is a misunderstanding.

Clergy: Clarify your position in terms of being head of staff. Do you welcome opinions that differ from your own? Do you support individual creativity? Do you want a musician who will be a pastoral presence as well as a musician? Or do you want someone who is just good enough at their job and who will not be too popular with the congregation, someone who will do only what is asked of them and who won't get involved in matters of the wider church that are not directly related to the music program?

Lack of Flexiblity

Flexibility is necessary for both parties. There is probably not a week that goes by in our services at the Wesley Seminary Chapel that I don't say, "Flexibility is my middle name"—and that's true. Things just don't always happen the way they're supposed to happen, or the way we planned for them to happen. There can be misprints in the bulletin, something might get skipped in the service, the soloist has a sore throat and we have to find someone else to sing at the last minute, or the public address or projection systems are not working right. We cannot allow ourselves to get derailed, or even irritated, by these things.

More broadly, musicians might be asked to play a style of music that is out of their comfort zone, or to bring music into worship that might not be the genre they prefer. There are just too many occasions to list that call for flexibility—but without it, we're sunk.

Inability to Compromise

We each bring different things to the table when it comes to doing worship together. We earlier discussed the ways clergy and musicians are different, not only in our training but also in our style of work and our world view. The most productive way to negotiate these differences is through compromise. Ideally, we work at issues together and we find solutions that are mutually acceptable; no one is pulling rank and the discussions are open and honest.

Strategies for Dealing with Conflict

Is It Worth It?

There are healthy ways and less healthy ways to approach conflict. Coffman writes in *Work and Peace* that the emotions most operative in conflict—anger and fear—often operate simultaneously. "Two or more people beset by anger and fear will fuel each other's fire, and the conflict will escalate."[3] If one party does not stop to cool down, trouble quickly ensues, because "an adrenalin rush in one being can precipitate or accentuate an adrenalin rush in another.... The emotions of one individual and the escalating emotional reaction of another" are connected.[4]

When there is a serious misunderstanding, there are several sets of strategies for dealing with conflict in a way that has a chance of producing a desirable outcome. Despite overlapping aspects, each set of strategies has a distinctive approach that could make it the best-suited to a particular situation.

First, decide if a source of conflict is serious enough to warrant pursuing it. "I AM Worth it" is an acronym used by Redford Williams, a professor of psychiatry and medicine at Duke University, to help one decide about whether or not to call attention to a matter.

- is it **I**mportant (does it really matter?)
- is it **A**ppropriate (is it reasonable to feel this way?)
- is it **M**odifiable (can anything about the situation actually be changed?)
- is it **W**orth addressing?

If any of these questions produces a "no" answer, then it is not an issue worth addressing. Dr. Williams says, however, that if the answer is "yes" to all four, then press ahead.[5]

Understanding Personality Styles

It will come as no surprise that different personality styles approach conflict in different ways. In their book *Speaking the Truth in Love,* Kenneth C. Haugk and Ruth Koch identify these approaches as:

- *passive*—keeps quiet and, although feelings have been hurt, doesn't deal with the situation
- *aggressive*—pushes back, verbally attacking or putting down the person who has upset them
- *passive-aggressive*—talks to a third party, involving and upsetting them as well; may pout or cry in an attempt to manipulate the other person
- *assertive*—deals with the situation. "Assertive behavior is a constructive way of living and relating to other people. It is behavior that reflects concern about being honest, direct, open, and natural in relations with others."[6] This is the style that's most likely to allow for the creation and maintenance of healthy relationships

Dealing with Conflict Starts with Oneself

In *The Resilience Factor: Seven Essential Skills for Overcoming Life's Inevitable Obstacles,* Karen Reivich and Andrew Shatte provide guidelines for changing one's mind-set in order to deal effectively with conflict. Here is a summary of their suggestions:

1. *Your thinking affects your behavior:* Whether you think you can't or you think you can, both are right. Do not limit your ability with imagined obstacles.
2. *Avoid thinking traps:* Do not automatically blame yourself when things go wrong, and do not jump to conclusions.
3. *Detect icebergs:* Know situations that may make you overreact.
4. *Challenge beliefs:* Understand why you think the way you do so you can break out of old paradigms and search for new solutions.
5. *Put it in perspective:* Don't waste time worrying about what might be—get the facts.
6. *Calm yourself:* Calm your emotions so you can deal with the problem at hand.
7. *Real-time resilience:* Learn to convert counterproductive thoughts into productive ones.[7]

Levels of Conflict Resolution

When members of the team get into conflict with each other, if possible, get a commitment from them to talk privately in the same room. There are several levels of interaction; try to facilitate the process to deal at Level 1 or 2. Each time we move down the list we lose control in our lives by losing control of the final decision, so deal with it early! Effective leaders train themselves and their team members to address the earliest sign of conflict. Dr. Jim R. Wadford, executive coach and consultant in Charlotte, North Carolina, has developed the following description of the stages of conflict.[8]

Level 1: Some will be willing to talk one-to-one (dialogical problem solving)—best.

Level 2: Two people ask for third party intervention—a mediation.

Level 3: Two people are so angry they can't talk directly and can only talk individually to a mediator.

Level 4: Some people are so conflicted that they need another person to work out the solution—an arbitrator.

Level 5: Very serious conflict that may lead to litigation.

Disarming Techniques

When someone comes at you with angry words and/or accusations, use the following pattern for disarming the anger so that it is possible to have a meaningful conversation:[9]

- Agree on something (do not equivocate)
- Say, "It must make you feel…"
- Next say, "Tell me more about…"
- Next say, "How do we handle this?" and/or "What is your suggestion to make it right?"
- Next say, "It makes me feel ________ that this has happened."

Using these disarming techniques may allow you to go deeper and be able to identify the actual real problem and get to its causes. Ballou makes the following additional suggestions:

- When someone approaches you with criticism, reframe the criticism (only in your mind)—think of it merely as a request for information.
- Listen carefully to the words and note the choice of words and the inflection in their voice.
- Look for emotional cues to understand how they feel.
- Let others finish talking before you respond. It is OK to have some silence between their words and your response. Do not be guilty of forming your next point while they are still talking. They will know that you have not listened to their issues and did not understand their feelings. Silence is your friend. It offers an opportunity to clarify the situation. Listen before you respond, letting the silence clear the air and give importance to their comments.
- Thank them for coming to you with their comments. Repeat what you understood them to say, to see if you have heard them correctly.
- Ask for their suggestions for resolution. This will let you know if they really want the situation resolved or just want to complain.

- Give them any relevant information on the subject and any other background information as to why this situation exists. Thank them again for talking.
- Pay attention to them—this is an opportunity for ministry. Keep in mind the possibility that there may be a personal crisis behind the emotion, and their problem may have nothing to do with the words coming out of their mouth.
- Be sensitive and caring as you choose to educate and provide care to this person, who may possibly be in need.

Having Healthy Conversations

Here are additional thoughts on healthy conflict resolution shared by a colleague who works with church staff mediation and churches in crisis.

Our language can defeat our goals and distort the understanding of important issues. For that reason all church leaders—both staff and laity—can benefit from agreeing to abide by guidelines to ensure healthy conversations during discussions where strong feelings are being expressed. Conflict often becomes destructive when people act and speak based on feelings of anxiety, fear, isolation (not belonging), we vs. them, and being out of control.

Yet, feelings are natural responses when we are engaged in a disagreement. The hope is to create an environment where people speak, listen, and act, informed by their feelings. It is important to provide time and space for feelings to be expressed, to accept the person's right to feel as they do, and to love the person who is angry, sad, or scared.

A Possible Agenda

My colleague also suggests the following general agenda for a meeting to resolve significant conflict. She credits inspiration from the church leadership authority Gil Rendle and offers these as starting points before the actual conflict discussion begins.

1. In a spirit of reflection and Scriptural grounding:
    - Stop trying to solve problems and trying to fix people. Don't be problem-focused, but focus on where positive passion and energy shows up.
    - Get to know yourself so that you can be constant in purpose but flexible in strategy.

- Do not confuse the difference between description and evaluation. Strive to focus the conversation on issues that matter and do not make judgments that stop the conversation.
- Focus on what God wants you to do—and what that looks like.
- Do not overlook the power of a good question.
- Trust comes from communication with as much transparency as possible.

2. Agree to basic ground rules for working through conflict such as these Twelve Ground Rules.

Twelve Ground Rules for Working through Conflict

1. Speak for yourself, not for others.
2. Challenge another's behaviors or ideas, but not his/her motives or worth.
3. No blaming
4. No labeling
5. No threats
6. Send "I" messages rather than "You" messages.
7. Propose the change you want rather than just talking about what you don't like. Be specific and descriptive.
8. Acknowledge your share in creating the conflict or tension.
9. Respect and explore differing experiences of the same event.
10. Evaluate in terms of "costs and benefits" rather than "good and evil." Evaluate in terms of "needs and interests" rather than "right and wrong."
11. No interrupting. Care enough to listen before you respond. Respond to show understanding of the other before stating your position.
12. Describe feelings rather than acting them out or trying to disguise them.

3. Identify a shared goal, something like:

> Our shared goal in this conversation is to focus on how we can most effectively and meaningfully serve God and this church as members of our shared staff team, with respect for our different ministries and responsibilities, and in an environment where we can thrive and do our best work.

4. Identify individual goals as well.
5. Name specific options any of the participants would like to put on the table for consideration.
6. Choose which option you will put energy into developing in today's conversation with the goal of leaving with a specific common understanding of direction and expectations.
7. Agree on next steps.

Tips Inspired by the Book *Difficult Conversations*

Stress, misunderstandings, frustration, and anger—they can all cause us to need to have a conversation that is one we would probably rather not have, but which is essential. You have been accused of not doing your job. Someone has called you a diva and said that you have no concern for the whole church, but care only about the music. The clergy has criticized you for not using enough world music in services, when you know that there has been global music in every service for the last three months.

Plan the Conversation

Just as we would prepare for a church service or rehearsal, *plan the conversation* ahead of time. The authors of the book *Difficult Conversations*[10] suggest being clear on questions such as:

- What took place that caused this conflict?
- What has been the impact on me?
- What do I hope to accomplish if I have this conversation?
- Are there "hot buttons" I need to think about for myself or the other person?
- Am I bringing an attitude to the conversation that can affect its outcome?
- Am I making assumptions about the other person's reaction to the conversation?
- What about my sense of myself depends upon the way this conversation goes?

Have the Conversation

Again, just as for a recital or a service, *practice the conversation*. Mentally rehearse it or practice it out loud with a trusted friend. Now, *have the conversation,* no matter how much you would like to avoid it. Realize that, if the conversation really needs to take place, avoiding it only makes the situation worse. What we say matters, but how we say it matters even more. And the goal is, as the *Prayer of St. Francis* asks, "that [we] may not so much seek to be understood as to understand."

- Say why you are bringing this issue forward at this time and say you hope that together we can find a solution.
- Acknowledge that there are two sides to this and every story—and that the problem is not with your views, but the difference between your views.
- Listen to hear their view of the situation.
- Ask questions to clarify that you understand what they have said.
- Make neutral responses, such as *This seems very important to you* or *So what you are thinking is…?*
- Try to figure out how this misunderstanding arose in the first place.
- Keep focused on issues and not on marginal factors that can distract you.
- Begin conversations with objective statements about what happened and how you felt about it. Start with *I'd like to talk to you about…*; *Can you tell me more about…*; *I'm interested in your take on…*; *I think we may have different views on….*

Problem-Solve

- Identify options: what next steps will meet both your needs? Acting on the premise that you both care about your relationship and want it to continue, what will work for you both?
- What would be the ideal action that would happen next? Each of you may have a different view of what is ideal in this case, so discuss it and arrive at a solution that seems workable, and also discuss the time frame.
- Commit to trying another strategy if the initial one fails to work.

- Commit to keeping communication open and to checking in with each other when anything troubling or confusing arises again.

I hope that you find a strategy to follow from the various techniques listed above, one that will work for you and allow you to enjoy a healthy relationship with your colleagues in ministry.

Notes

1. Lawson, 46.

2. Hugh Ballou, *Creating and Sustaining Healthy Teams: Preventing and Managing Team Conflict,* Blacksburg: SynerVision Internation, Inc., 2011, [e-book], 5.

3. James R. Coffman, *Work and Peace in Academe: Leveraging Time, Money, and Intellectual Energy through Managing Conflict,* Bolton, MA: Anker Publishing Company, Inc., 2005, 124.

4. *Ibid.,* 125.

5. *Consumer Reports on Health* 23, no. 10 (October, 2011): 6.

6. Ruth N. Koch and Kenneth C. Haugt, *Speaking the Truth in Love,* St. Louis: Stephen Ministries, 1992, 23.

7. Ballou, *Creating and Sustaining,* 13.

8. *Ibid.,* 12.

9. *Ibid.*, 14–15.

10. Douglas Stone, Bruce Patton, and Sheila Heden, *Difficult Conversations: How to Discuss What Matters Most,* New York: Penguin Books, 1999.

8

Why Musicians Leave

Resign? The empirical evidence says that was the last thing she wanted to do. Her ministry, her congregational family, and her choir family were a huge part of her life. She was beloved and admired by everyone inside and outside of the church. She was deeply committed to the church and its mission. She was dedicated to improving her art; she was a consummate professional; and she was, of course, very attached to the organ she helped design and whose installation she oversaw. Why would she resign after so many years and while she was still well within her prime?

—e-mail to author

Why is the musician most often the one who leaves when the situation becomes unmanageable? Musicians are the ones who leave because of the uneven distribution of power inherent in the hierarchical system that governs most churches, which can manifest itself in many ways. What follows is my breakdown of the specific types of problems that can make an environment so intolerable that taking oneself out of it may be the only option.

Reasons Musicians Leave

Hostile Work Environment

On occasion, the situation becomes so tense and so toxic that the musician becomes physically ill and needs to leave for the sake of physical health and emotional well-being. A hostile environment is not conducive to productive ministry, especially when many staff members have been systematically forced out or outright fired. Here are the testimonies of several musicians who have endured this pain:

> I have worked with many people in my career, and I had never encountered anyone with whom I couldn't work. All that changed with this senior pastor and the number of lives he ruined. Person after person left (voluntarily, or was fired)—it was just not a good place to work any longer.
>
> ❧
>
> I tried everything I knew to make it work, to the point of working with a coach to enable better communication between the clergy and myself—in order to allow me to feel that I wanted to stay. But the toxicity of the environment and the emotional abuse that so many of us experienced rose to a level that was just something I couldn't continue to endure.
>
> ❧
>
> It's difficult to work in a situation when all my former colleagues have left or been fired: many of the "second hires" are also gone—a total of thirty people left the staff in a period of only a few years. I can't tell you how difficult it was to remain working there, but I did so as long as I could stand it.
>
> ❧
>
> There's no staff that will ever be perfect—none—because we're human. But if we have a concern for justice for day laborers and the homeless, it seems that the same concern could be extended to the staff!

One retired professional manager at a large corporation expressed amazement at the short-sightedness demonstrated by one church.

> Every management class I took encouraged managers to "hire up" to advance their mission. That is, one should hire people who were far smarter and more talented than you. Such people might be more challenging to manage, but they would be the real difference makers. That is what I and my colleagues did, and it worked. There are very, very few [such musicians] around the country and to drive her out instead of nurturing her ministry and integrating it into new directions for the church was indeed reprehensible if not totally misguided. Incredibly, this musician came to believe her only choice was to leave a toxic staff environment where she was not appreciated and where she was no longer welcome.

There are times when the toxic environment presents a moral question. We are human beings working within social systems and, like the Hoberman sphere, we are interrelated. Never heard of the Hoberman sphere? It is an expandable device (some might call it a toy) that provides a wonderful analogy for the interconnectedness of individuals on a team. Expand one place on the sphere, there is contraction in another place, and the entire system is affected with every change. Church staff members are interrelated just like points on the sphere. How one staff member is treated in a meeting affects the morale of the other members of the staff. Similarly, when staff members leave or are fired, this too, affects the entire staff. As one colleague e-mailed me:

> I am trying to figure out if I can continue to do ministry with someone who can say something to another colleague like "you have done nothing for the church in your three years here" and "It's not the church's fault you have a child." How can I continue to work in a place where they might as well install a revolving door for easier exit by the number of staff who have left since this pastor came? Do I have a moral responsibility here? Or do I just keep trying to do music and worship and continue to keep my mouth shut?

Another musician asked: "How many staff people's lives do we have to chew up before we say 'enough already'?"

Psychological Coercion

Many consider churches a place where employees will be respected and treated fairly, a place where they can work without feeling coerced or bullied. It is shocking to find out that this is not always the case.

Writing about workplace abuse of staff, John K. Setser refers to social scientist Albert Biderman's description of such psychological pressure as "a process by which the target's thought and behavior is altered, causing the individual's will to be broken."[1] In such situations, independent thinking is discouraged and a staff member's ideas are repudiated if they are different from, or have not been originated by, the senior pastor.

Sometimes it takes the form of intimidation in staff meetings, when a pastor calls a staff member to task in an angry, accusatory way. Other times it is more private. One musician was subjected to individual "supervision sessions" in place of staff meetings, so that the senior pastor could manipulate the musician out of the eyes and ears of other staff members.

Even threats are part of this coercion, as when one highly respected musician was threatened with being "brought up on charges" by the personnel committee for perceived failure to accept a new staffing model, one that had never been explained. He was accused of being oppositional because he simply did not understand how it was supposed to work.

The effects of psychological coercion are just as harmful as physical torture. Its victims "have a tendency to deny, minimize, rationalize, and intellectualize their mistreatment. They simply cannot bring themselves to believe that something bad is happening to them."[2]

For example, an abused musician who dismisses the need to meet with the personnel committee to discuss the toxic work environment is actually denying the problem and choosing to avoid conflict. In his heart, he confesses to entertaining thoughts that no musician ever wins in a conflict between musician and clergy. In these situations, victims may blame themselves, saying: "I figured there was something wrong with me. I have never met anybody I couldn't work with before."

Manipulation of people and situations are part of psychological coercion, such as that exercised by a senior pastor who tried to persuade the departing musician to buy in to plans being made for handling the music program after the musician's departure:

> What I'm looking for is your endorsement, if you will. This needs to seem to be your idea, as we discussed, if people are going to receive these events and your absence well. Please try to think how you can help us sell these special musical opportunities.

Feeling Patronized and Demeaned

In such abusive situations, staff members may be attacked for not supporting the minister's vision if they raise questions or even if they ask questions of clarification. Part of the picture is constant criticism not just for a particular task that was done, but also for the way it was handled. Musicians report feeling that there seems to be no value placed on the quality of their work, just on how well they play the game, even when it is difficult to figure out how the game should be played.

> It was insulting to be taken to task simply for the way I asked a question, or worded an email—the questions were asked in good faith, and I was never demeaning or rude. I just never figured out what kind of

questions could be asked, of whom, and in what circumstances. This ambiguity goes back a number of years, judging by dates on messages in my e-mail box.

It felt like both the clergy were totally ganging up on me the way they had clearly rehearsed their parts and were in lock-step on the issues—none of which had been issues with any other clergy before. How can I suddenly be a complete idiot when it comes to people? I am approaching the "fed-up" stage. I really have no desire to be in a room with either of them again. If my mortgage refinancing were approved, I'd clear out my office tonight. In truth, I feel more like a fool (for willingly submitting to this abuse) than a trooper.

Lack of Clarity on Accountability

It is easy to see how difficult it can be when lines of authority are not clear, especially if the musician doesn't know to whom s/he is responsible: Clergy only? Clergy and worship/music committee? Clergy, music/worship committees *and* personnel committee? And for what precisely is the musician to be held accountable? Timeliness in arriving at staff meetings? Tempo of the hymns? Following-up on a potential choir member? Cleanliness of his desk?

It is inexplicable to me why more value seems to be placed on the accountability factor than on the work actually being accomplished. "The clergy have a greater desire," one musician writes, "to hold me accountable than to plan worship—including all of the services in Holy Week. I'm asked to apologize even when I have done nothing wrong: 'accepting accountability' is the senior pastor's term—whatever that really means."

Hypocrisy

There are difficulties when trust is eroded, and even more difficulties when the senior pastor is out-and-out hypocritical. One example is an unwillingness to apply to daily life the sermons the clergy preach, particularly with respect to their relationship with musicians. One e-mail to the musician basically cautioned the musician not to take too seriously anything said from the pulpit, particularly warning that the contents of the sermon should not be thought of as applying to their working relationship.

Philosophical and Theological Differences

Important questions of institutional identity can be a cause of problems. Is the church a business, a corporate structure, a non-profit? Is it a family, a community, a loose collection of individuals and nothing more? These identities portray fundamental differences in terms of nearly everything having to do with the way church boards, vestries, staff, committees, and other groups operate.

When senior pastors adopt a corporate model rather than a servant leadership model, they attempt to measure their effectiveness by the standards of Wall Street rather than spiritual ones. As Setser argues:

> A corporate mandate is appropriate if the goal is measureable success; not so if the goal is to love God and serve people. This is because the aim of a corporate mandate is, above all else, to benefit the organization. Success for these organizations is defined in financial, material, and numeric terms. The feelings, hopes, and needs of people are of little consequence under this mandate.[3]

Another musician has written, "Our concepts of church as Body of Christ differ; I believe it's a holistic organism; the senior pastor and the associate believe it's a corporate, hierarchical organizational structure."

The church-as-corporation model asks the question, "How can we get more members?" rather than "How can we serve the members and the community better?" or "How can we enlarge the budget?" rather than "Where is God calling this church? In what ministries does the church most need to be involved?" Goals such as bigger budgets, new or bigger buildings, or more worship services can get in the way of the servant ministry to which we are called. In these situations, the survival of the institution assumes greater importance than the true mission of the church. "Once the door is open for ministerial success to be equated with a measurable outcome, a spiritual paradigm is lost.... The senior pastor's job title, likewise, changes from shepherd and teacher to president and CEO."[4] One musician reports that, with his senior pastor, "process is indeed more important than people; it was true in his first months at the church and, several years later, remains true today."

Lack of Clarity about One's Job

Although having clarity about one's duties seems so obvious, the lack of it is often a potent cause of conflict in many situations. What is expected of the musician? If additional choirs or services are added, will the salary be adjusted accordingly? Who calls the substitute if the musician is sick? Does the musician on staff have right of first refusal for a wedding or a funeral, or does the clergy contact other organists to play? Is the organist expected to play for wedding rehearsals? Organists have been known to arrive at church to practice, only to find that they were expected to have been there earlier for the wedding rehearsal or, as in one case, they were supposed to have been playing for a special worship service then in progress but about which they had never been informed.

Who does the service planning? Is there a meeting where worship is planned? Does the senior pastor do it all or is there consultation and team planning? Does the musician give information to someone else on the staff to be typed, or does the musician prepare the bulletin as well?

One musician was accused of not being a team player because he was not helping the church secretary, something he had never known he was supposed to be doing in the first place. "It's clear my job has changed," e-mailed a colleague, "but I have received no updated job description, even after requesting it many times. And now I am being evaluated on tasks for which I never knew I was responsible." Yet, too often, when musicians ask for job clarification or inquire about the customary ways of the church, they are perceived as being difficult and uncooperative. Sometimes they may even be threatened with dismissal for simply having suggested a different way of doing something. Implausible as it seems, musicians report not having been consulted in any way when a personnel committee has decided to change their job description or add worship services or choirs without consultation. "A new associate is now doing my job as worship planner," complains one musician, "but there has been no conversation about this change and it was a complete surprise to me." Worship committees have been known to decide to split the job into two positions and hire someone else for the other half, without ever discussing it with the person currently holding the position. Similarly, it seems only courteous to contact the personnel involved should their office need to be moved, or if church policy changes and they are affected. One organist was accused of insubordination for having told the bride that the check was to be mailed to him directly, not realizing that the pastor had changed the policy so that now wedding couples wrote out a single check to the church for all services.

Lack of Clarity about the Musician's Relationship to the Church

Should a musician be a member of the church? Is church membership required? Or is it forbidden? What about pledging? Sometimes musicians are asked to pledge, even to tithe, and sometimes it is even written into their contracts. One organist in the Midwest was subjected to criticism and threatened with dismissal when he got behind on his pledge. (No, I'm not making this up!)

Differences in Work Style

Clergy and musicians simply do not always operate within the same time frame or with the same sense of urgency. Differences in work style come into play when one is a workaholic and the other is laid back. The workaholic never thinks the other person is really working hard enough.

I believe, however, the most significant difference relates to the amount of notice musicians receive from clergy when it comes to worship planning. Musicians need to know the sermon theme and scripture in order to select music that will fit with the service, and they need more notice than clergy might realize. The musician is working with a host of ensembles whose members have varying skills, and they need adequate time to prepare the music. I can tell you from experience that choirs want to do a good job, and they get really grumpy when they do not have sufficient rehearsal on a piece of music. If the music is not already in the library, the musician needs sufficient lead time to order it. One seminary-trained musician writes:

> The thing I appreciate most is getting the sermon topic and scripture lessons far enough in advance that I can plan the hymns and service music to fit. I select anthems far in advance by the church year, but sometimes I can move them about when they fit better with another service.
>
> We're not just musicians, we are church musicians. We study for our craft just as seminary graduates do. (I'm a seminary graduate myself.) The more you can share with the musicians, the better the service will be. To me there is no better evangelism than a quality service. The people know the care that went into preparing it.[5]

Boundary Issues

An overly-personal encounter or an unwelcome romantic overture cannot help but create a difficult situation on a church staff. While this is inappropriate in any workplace, it is particularly untenable in a church setting. It is always possible that one party is reading the other's signals incorrectly, and it is important to get clarity on that. If it truly is an issue of harassment, then it needs to be reported immediately. If there is evidence or even the appearance of impropriety or sexual abuse involving a minor, every staff member has a clear legal obligation to report such information to the appropriate authorities. "If you see something, say something" applies to these situations as well as those in TSA's Homeland Security bulletins.

Lack of Respect for Music's Role in Worship or for the Musician

We are in music because we believe in its power to affect lives as the Word of God is transmitted through the music we play, sing, or conduct. We are church musicians because we love music, we feel called to this ministry, and we feel we can make a difference. When we are not respected personally or as musicians, or when our program is not valued, it is pretty much a deal breaker.

> I am confused and hurt: I have worked to build an excellent program and kept it growing for many years. I am respected by colleagues and appreciated by the choir and congregation, but apparently, not by the clergy. I feel I am being forced out because my emails weren't worded to the clergy's satisfaction.

When we are not respected personally or as musicians, or when our program is not valued, it is pretty much a deal breaker.

Another factor contributing to clerical antipathy toward music may be as small as a minister having been informed early in life that he or she cannot sing. This seemingly insignificant incident—shame on the perpetrator!—can create an antipathy toward music or the musician. At the least, it can cause a lingering ambivalence about music on the part of the clergy.

Failure of Parties to Acknowledge Mutual Accountability

> There is absolutely no acknowledgement of a two-way street. The senior pastor and associate take no responsibility for this situation and feel that everything is my fault.

> I think this is the last straw—I can't seem to do anything right and am trying to figure out how to make it through rehearsal.

As Weiser effectively explored in his book, *Healers: Harmed and Harmful,* issues that are always claimed to be "the other person's fault"—a key characteristic of dysfunctional individuals—can cause the relationship to derail.

> This situation was not just a matter of the clergy's wanting to hold you accountable and your being sensitive to how he does that. The issues are far more complex in that there is lack of awareness on the clergy's part of how they have contributed in the past and continue to contribute to the stress and pain. Despite the efforts I believe the clergy have made, they continue to oversimplify the issue as a systemic problem of accountability instead of a systemic challenge re: understanding how language and assumptions and back story operate to erode trust. It is almost impossible to rebuild this trust without lots of intervention, commitment to

> change oneself, patience for patterns to change, and energy. I see exhaustion, and I don't hear/see adequate commitment to put in the tremendous effort it would take to turn things around.[6]

Attempts to Control Musicians

"Senior pastor dominance," writes Dr. Setser, "results in staff associates having to promote the senior leaders' agenda. Such dominance stifles creativity and constricts the wisdom of God. Matthew 19:19b implies that wisdom is justified by all her children, not just senior leaders."[7]

Chain of command is part of the *modus operandi* of this hierarchical structure. In some churches you can only talk to your supervisor, who then takes the issue up the corporate ladder, all to ensure control by those at the top. The problem comes when this structure is not adequately explained to the staff. One pastor is reported to have been furious when a leaking pipe in the choir room was brought to the attention of a trustee walking through after church, rather than to the attention of the pastor, who happened to be out of town at the time.

The need for control on the part of the clergy manifests itself in the urge to micromanage: "The tone of every conversation, every e-mail, even the look on my face," complains one musician, "was scrutinized and held to account—and it's just not possible to be creative or even to minister at all in that kind of environment." One musician reports that suddenly conversation with the head of the personnel committee was forbidden, although such interaction had been the practice of the church and was permitted in the church's operating procedures. Another reports being limited in interaction with members of the congregation, even to the point of not being allowed to provide support to families in crisis or hospitalized members of the choir, both appropriate interaction between musician and parishioners under normal circumstances. Still another reports that the pastor attempted to script responses to particular issues facing the church, seeing staff members as public relations automatons rather than as creative individuals with their own opinions.

Insecure leaders don't want to share power because of their desire or need to control everything within their sphere of influence. Thomas L. Are describes the consequences of the controlling personality:

> The thing about Tom's ego is, it is a cover-up. He is not that self-confident. Sometimes he feels like a little boy trying to fill a man's role. Inside he is afraid. To keep himself from failure or exposure, he "plays

> his power." He is the manager. David, whom he respects as a competent musician, is one of those whom he must manage...
>
> He has decided that they will have a role relationship. That means Tom = manager, David = managee. Tom will have to protect both his domain and his ego. Anything else would require a lot of trust and love and communication.[8]

Lovett Weems, in his study of church leadership, talks about an "expandable pie," where the ability to influence is not fixed in a way that one may have more only at the expense of another, who must have less. "The expandable power pie concept, however," he explains, "leads to greater reciprocity of influence and a reduced need to protect one's own territory.... The more power a leader is willing to entrust to others, the more others are willing to grant influence and power to the leader. Therefore, as others grow stronger, the leader's influence with them is increased."[9] How ironic! The very influence such controlling clergy crave could be achieved harmlessly, simply by a 180-degree shift in their attitude!

Note: Musicians, too, have control issues, addressed in Chapter 1 in the section, "We can be our own worst enemies."

Jealousy

Church musicians on staff when a new pastor arrives can provide valuable insight into the culture of the congregation. However, sometimes newly arriving clergy do not appreciate this resource and may actually feel jealous, especially if the musician has been in the parish for a long time and is well-liked. The newly arrived minister can learn a lot about the congregation from the musician, who has spent years getting to know the people, their passions, what upsets them, and what energizes them. But this same knowledge can also be perceived as a threat.

Charlotte Kroeker addresses a different aspect of jealousy in *The Sounds of Our Offerings*. "Pastors may not know how to deal with the strong responses music [elicits from] the congregation in worship. I asked one of the pastors trained in music about the phenomenon. His response: 'I think all of us who preach secretly wish that our words had the power of music. If only we could understand and appreciate that power and use it in the best sense.' "[10]

Another factor, frankly, is simple envy when the music program is praised. Clergy can feel threatened. A choir member wrote, probably tongue-in-cheek, to a musician who had left a difficult church situation: "Didn't you know the Eleventh Commandment? *Thou shalt not be a star before me.*"

Desire for Change

Pastorally-initiated changes in any aspect of the music program may strike the congregation as an attack on the musician or the music program itself. Discussion about a new hymnal, a different service time, or alternative service style has the potential to be a source of conflict. So does the choice of music genre. That's a big one, as there are many situations where the differences in musical preference are profound. On the flip side, pastors may see musicians as obstacles to change and thus not include musicians in these discussions, even when the subject relates to their area of responsibility. Musicians rightfully expect to be included in discussions about music and worship and resent being excluded from major decisions affecting the music and worship life of the church they serve.

Difference in Denominational Traditions

Clergy who are now serving a church different from the one in which they were raised can bring a set of expectations and practices that are out of sync with the staff or the church.[11] As a corollary, musicians who come out of a different denomination can bring a different (and sometimes unwelcome) perspective to their current position. They have also been known to receive criticism for their choice of music (and even music publishers!). "That's Catholic music," was the charge when the musician in a Protestant church ordered from a certain publisher.

Educational Differences

Some clergy have substantial musical training; many more have little musical experience. Even fewer musicians have theological training. Consequently, we do not speak each other's language. Problems also arise when the musician has higher educational degrees than the clergy. This can translate into pastoral jealousy with an attendant negative impact on the possibility of a collegial working relationship. This is particularly true if the musician tends to use this difference to gain advantage or influence.

Calling

A fundamental commonality between clergy and church musicians is their sense of having been called to ministry. It can also be a key point in conflict. While musicians often also feel called to their vocation, the clergy—from seminary orientation through ordination—may not only feel called, but often may believe that their vision is more valid than anybody else's because *they* are following God's calling. According to Kroeker, "Clergy who see conflict as an issue said their vocations were initiated by a personal call rather than as a result of encouragement by a mentor or other individual in close relationship to them over a long period of time. These clergy tended toward more authoritarian leadership styles and were more likely to claim the authority of their position in making decisions, pulling rank when disagreements arose."[12] Mutual acknowledgment that both feel called can help alleviate this as a source of tension.

Lack of Communication

As was pointed out earlier, it is fruitless at best and disastrous at worst when issues of conflict are not discussed. If issues aren't put on the table early when things are not going well, it is more than possible that there will be no turning back once the discussion does take place.

"He has encoded expectations," a friend of mine wrote me, "but unless they're made explicit, how can I know what he has in mind? It seems to be a prime example of something like 'process over people.'" Expectations should be shared, not hidden. Conflicts or complaints should be aired and resolved. All staff evaluations, particularly those with potentially negative consequences, need to be both oral and written, and accompanied by a clear time table for improvement and subsequent re-evaluation. Termination should only be considered if the staff member is unwilling or unable to address the church's formally communicated concerns. No musician should ever be surprised by termination, yet there are numerous cases where this is precisely what has happened.

Should You Leave?

Sometimes it just does not work any longer We need to know when we and the job are no longer a fit. As Paul Westermeyer writes:

> If you as the church musician are pushed around by a manipulative pastor, or if one family in the church starts to control your choice of music, you have a bad compromise or no compromise at all. You cannot contribute your talents in such a situation because you are again reduced to being a music grinder or hired chattel. Even if you analyzed the fit as carefully as possible before you came, you may early or late discover that you did not analyze well enough. You may have to

> leave. You do not do this lightly, you do not do it without face-to-face discussions and meetings, and you do it with deep regret. But do it you must so that you can move to a place where serving the Lord and serving the people is possible.[13]

In her book, *Preaching to the Choir,* Victoria Sirota offers these questions to help the discernment process as one decides whether or not to leave.

- Is this the same job that I felt called to when I came? What has changed?
- Do I trust the clergy? Can I have professional and honest conversation about changes in liturgy and worship style?
- Are my gifts being used well in this situation?
- Does the music program complement the other ministries of the church? Or is there a disconnect?
- Am I interested in learning a new musical style? Is the congregation open to blended services, or do they wish to change over completely to a new style?
- Are there funds available to hire additional people to play the new music or to cover the costs of my studying to broaden my skills?
- Do I feel respected by those in authority, or am I made to feel inadequate despite my education, training, background, and experience?
- What would I lose by leaving this position? Would I grieve inconsolably? Do I feel called to new areas of growth in this place?
- Conversely, what would I gain by leaving this position? Would it feel like a great weight had been lifted from my shoulders?[14]

One staff member writes:

> I was good at my job and people liked me, which was fine until my popularity caught the notice of the senior pastor. One day out of the blue, he asked me why I was trying to steal the church away from him. I was stunned and told him I would never do such a thing. He listened, but refused to believe me. From that moment on, it was as if I was [sic] dead to him. He publicly questioned my character and doubted my calling. I became tentative and watchful. I was careful to say and do only the things I thought would please him. However, instead of approval I received blank looks and a cold shoulder. Finally, I offered my resignation. In response he simply told me that I had made a wise decision.[15]

Many factors enter into the decision to make a change, especially if this is a position that you have held for a significant period of time and where you have felt that your ministry was rewarding for you and having a positive impact on the congregation.

Sometimes, it's just time to leave.

Notes

1. Setser, 69.
2. *Ibid.,* 74.
3. *Ibid.,* 38.
4. *Ibid.,* 43.
5. Gerald Piercey, e-mail to author, September 22, 2009.
6. [Name withheld], e-mail to author, April 26, 2007.
7. Setser, 51.
8. Are, 35.
9. Weems, 67.
10. Krocker, 217.
11. *Ibid.,* 186.
12. *Ibid.*
13. Westermeyer, 29.
14. Victoria Sirota, *Preaching to the Choir: Claiming the Role of Sacred Musician,* New York: Church Publishing Incorporated, 2006, 125–126.
15. Setser, 9.

9

When the Musician Says Goodbye: Loss, Transition, and Starting Anew

Every time there are losses there are choices to be made. You choose to live your losses as passages to anger, blame, hatred, depression, and resentment or you choose to let these losses be passage to something new, something wider, and deeper.

—Henri Nouwen

Musicians leave their posts for any number of reasons in addition to those discussed in Chapter 8: a better-paying position, a church with a better choir, a better organ, more prestige. Some have out-grown their current position and crave one with more challenge. Others know another congregation well and prefer to be in ministry with them. However, leaving is not a solo act.

"Making a change in your career also impacts your personal life and those with whom you share it," writes life coach Cheryl Duerr. "They must be a part of your discernment process. Don't be surprised if changes happening to you at work precipitate changes in someone close to you. These changes might even further complicate what you are experiencing at work, and might at one or more times even derail the process. Don't be put off by this—it's a normal part of the process. If you expect it and are prepared for it, you'll be able to manage the disruption."[1]

People change jobs with increasing frequency these days. In a situation where there is no trauma or drama, leaving a church position can be pretty much like leaving any other job. Of course, one must be professional about the way the announcement is handled, giving appropriate notice (following contractual obligations to the letter), making the announcement, choosing a date for a farewell celebration if one is to be held, and packing up your books and music.

It is different, however, when a musician chooses to leave because the climate of the church has changed. This can happen for any number of reasons: the departure of a colleague with whom you have worked happily, the arrival of a new minister with whom you do not anticipate having an easy time, a change in church governance, a change in the direction of the church, or a new and unwelcome focus of the music program.

"Most people," writes John Maxwell, "change only when one of three things happens: they hurt enough that they have to, they learn enough that they want to, or they receive enough that they are able to."[2] The musicians I know who have left their church have done so primarily for the first reason—they hurt enough that they have to.

Either out of a sense of professionalism or imposed "vows of silence," a resignation may come as a surprise not only to the larger congregation, but also to those closest to the musician in the congregation. This produces frustration and anger, which may contribute to the negative impact on the church. In some churches, choir members have fled after a forced departure of the musician, and the congregations became shadows of their former selves due to this divisiveness.

This may happen not just because of the musician's departure, but also because of the way the matter is handled. When a veil of secrecy shrouds events, speculation runs high, leaving the congregation mired in innuendo and doubt, as this account from a colleague sadly demonstrates.

> During this pastor's tenure, I have witnessed the systematic dismembering of the spirit of the church through his (and personnel committee's) staffing actions. Now with his driving the musician from the church, in my opinion, he is excising the heart from what remains of that spirit. Given those beliefs, I am exercising the only means I have to vote my feelings, and that is to withdraw my membership, my financial pledge, and my talents.
>
> It bears saying that I had no inside information of what actually went on behind closed doors, not that I didn't try to find out starting two to three years ago when I first detected that the musician was suffering some anguish, though she was the last to admit or publicly show it.

> Everyone I asked, including the musician, refused to tell me anything and a number of staff cited an official "gag order" they were under that prevented them from talking. (What is that?) And, yes, I understand Human Resources privacy issues—but that doesn't make this situation any easier to understand, or accept.[3]

A Sense of Loss

> "Who are you?" said the Caterpillar....
>
> "I—I hardly know, sir, just at present," Alice replied rather shyly, "at least I know who I was when I got up this morning, but I think I just have been changed several times since then."
>
> Lewis Carroll, *Alice's Adventures in Wonderland*

This charming nineteenth-century English story describes the feelings many twenty-first century church musicians have when they leave a church position, particularly if they have served the church for a long time, and even more if they have been fulfilled in that ministry.

In situations where the leaving is involuntary—when a person is fired—the trauma can be substantial. Understandably there will be anger, hurt, possibly feelings of betrayal by the clergy and supporters in the congregation. My e-mail box is full of correspondence with people who have been involuntarily terminated. There really is a lot of hurt out there.

Regardless of the reasons for the musician's leaving, it can be very difficult. The degree of pain is likely directly proportional to the amount of time the musician has spent at that church and the degree of connection they have had with the congregation. When the musician feels compelled to leave the church (or is fired), the sense of loss to the individual is often incalculable, while the institutional degree of loss is often minimized. Statements such as these are attempts to gloss over that reality:

- She is going on to a better position, one that will use all her skills even more effectively.
- There's probably a better job out there, with a better choir and organ, and you deserve that.
- He is taking on more responsibility at [the new place of employment] and looking forward to new challenges and opportunities.

Statements by clergy often attempt to blame the musician:

- The musician didn't really fit my vision for the church any longer.
- The musician really wasn't a team player.
- The musician kept stepping over boundaries and insisting on making pastoral contacts when that's really my job.

All these rationalizations minimize the degree of the musician's loss—financial, yes, but also loss of community and sometimes of an entire social network. Often a musician's closest friends are in the church or in the choir. This can be accompanied by a fundamental loss of identity with the institutional church or with making music in the church, especially when the musician has served one place for a long time.

Musicians so closely identify with their work that it is a challenge to deal with one's self-identity when it has changed so fundamentally. Much has been written about lines of differentiation between our sense of self and our work. Still, with many musicians I know, they *are* their work. "This is who I am and what I do," they say, and it is hard to separate the two. "If I'm no longer a choir director or organist, who am I?" More generally, it may also be difficult not to be a leader any more, not to give the kind of support that you spent years giving, and not to receive affirmation as you had previously.

> I am so sad at not playing an important part in these people's lives any longer. From being able to influence the hearts and spirits of hundreds of people every week (choir and congregation) ... to being able to influence far fewer people in what feels like less significant ways amounts to another kind of loss.[4]

> I didn't realize how much my soul had been wounded by staying in the situation so long. I had to learn to trust in the clergy/musician relationship again. I had to learn to fan the embers that were left of my creativity to let them burn strong again. And I had to learn to be open to new situations not based on the pain and woundedness of the prior experience. That took time. Just changing church jobs does not mean that you have healed. You have to work at it for a long time. In my case, it was almost two years before I realized one day that it was good to be on a church staff and I found joy in my ministry once again.[5]

The loss may be surprisingly personal, as revealed in statements such as "I had a place in the columbarium of the church—I was going to be buried there." Or, "My daughter had planned to be married in that church, and now we cannot even drive by without feeling overwhelming waves of sadness." One musician's child, who had grown up in the church the parent has now left, said starkly: "They have ruined our life and our family."

The church year and music associated with particular liturgical festivals can trigger unexpected pain for departing musicians. "This is All Saints Sunday, one of the days that has meant the most to [our family]," despaired one musician. "We feel totally robbed of our roots and our extended family; our sense of our place as musicians who serve the church has been totally violated."

Stages in the Transition

> Now this is not the end. It is not even the beginning of the end. But it is, perhaps, the end of the beginning.
>
> Winston Churchill in the House of Commons
> November 10, 1942

Much can be learned about navigating the troubled waters of transition from William Bridges' book, *Making Sense of Life's Change: Transitions.* Typically people who experience major life changes identify "(1) an ending, followed by (2) a period of confusion and distress, leading to (3) a new beginning."[6] These stages may come in this order, simultaneously, or in a different sequence. Bridges notes that if a person has not willingly left a previous situation, it will be especially hard to accept the possibility that there might be a positive new beginning awaiting them.

Transitions begin with endings, and part of this is letting go of the life we have had in order to embrace the new. Yes, this is easier to say than to do, but entirely necessary. "We come to identify ourselves with the circumstances of our lives," says Bridges. "Who we think we are is partly defined by the roles and relationships that we have, both those we like and those we do not. But the bonds go deeper even than that. Our whole way of being, the personal style that makes you recognizably 'you' and me 'me' is developed within and adjusted to fit a given life pattern."[7]

There are strategies for looking at endings and getting a sense of how best to deal with them. Although an ending may be painful, or at least uncomfortable, endings are not always bad. However, they do lead to an in-between place that can be difficult to navigate, depending on the circumstances attached to the ending. Yes, the ending can be frightening, especially if it is a job loss with the financial impact on top of the emotional hit, but it can also be frightening when it includes a basic sense of loss of the fulfilling ministry that may not be easily replaced.

We may feel the impact more keenly when we are fired and did not see it coming, but the impact is nearly as great when we feel ambushed by events and decide we need to resign. Such endings can have an impact on our physical and emotional health, and steps need to be taken to mitigate those effects.

Bridges reminds us that endings often give new beginnings a place to take root and grow, once we have come to accept that our former self-image or long-held dreams are no longer operative, and that dwelling further on them may in fact be holding us back. This recommendation may be easier said than done, but it is essential to let go of the past if we are going to be able to move on into the future. Bridges shares his thoughts on four phases of the transition process, particularly on the way we approach "Endings."

Disengagement recalls the way Jesus went into the wilderness for forty days, or the tribal practice of youth separating themselves from their families and social structures by engaging in initiation ceremonies that usher them into their roles as adults. In this phase, we are disengaged from all the old familiar ways of looking at ourselves, our work, our friends. We're no longer the director of music at the Church of the Large Parking Lot, and in order to move forward we have to accept that.

Disidentification is a stage when our sense of identity is lost and we may not really know who we are any longer. "In most cases this disidentification process is really the inner side of the disengagement process. It is often particularly distressing in vocational transition, or in cases where the old roles and titles were an important part of the person's identity. The impact of such losses can be much greater than one imagines in advance."[8]

Disenchantment is a phase when things just are not the way they used to be and, because of that, nothing seems real. It may be a hard concept to wrap your brain around but, painful as it is, reflection on the old reality is necessary because "the mind is a vessel that must be emptied if new wine is to be put in."[9] Our culture tends to think of education and development as a process of building on what has gone before, consistently adding to the body of knowledge or skills that we already have acquired. Sometimes, however, we find it necessary to clean house, to get rid of assumptions and familiar ways of seeing our life. This is part of a transition into a new place. "The lesson of disenchantment begins with the discovery that in order to change—really to change, and not just to switch positions—you must realize that some significant part of your old reality was in your head, not out there."[10] That means that we have to shed the trappings of the previous position and acknowledge and name aspects of the job that were less than perfect and probably had been for a long time. "Maybe the job wasn't as great as I thought it was. Maybe I didn't really have the support I thought I had. Maybe I was being set up for failure and didn't realize it." This look into the rear-view mirror is both painful and necessary. Without this new perspective on our past experiences we can become disillusioned, and "while the disenchanted person moves on ... the disillusioned person stops and goes through the play again with new actors. Such a person is on a perpetual quest ... only [going] around in circles, and real movement and real development are arrested."[11]

Disorientation is the phase Bridges describes as one of "confusion and emptiness," where the comfortable and familiar now seems unreal, and when things in which we used to find meaning no longer matter. This is a neutral zone, a time out, and it is a necessary bridge for the next steps.[12]

There are parallels between these stages and Elisabeth Kubler-Ross's often-quoted steps in accepting death: denial, anger, bargaining, depression, and acceptance—not necessarily in that order. Endings really are quasi-death experiences, and they call on us to question who we are and whether we can not only survive, but also thrive again in a new situation. "In no rite or myth," wrote Mircea Eliade, the Romanian historian, philosopher, and professor, about tribal rituals, "do we find the initiatory death as something *final*, but always as the condition *sine qua non* of transition to another mode of being, a trial indispensable to regeneration; that is, to the beginning of a new life."[13] The musician who has had to leave a position is not the first to walk this path, but somehow hearing that does not make the road any easier.

To keep moving through the transition process, we need to accept the emptiness and embrace this time as an opportunity for self-renewal and reflection. We need to live in that space for a while as we prepare to start anew. "Endings and beginnings, with emptiness and germination in between. That is the shape of the transition periods in our lives, and these times come far more frequently in adulthood and cut far more deeply into it than most of us imagined that they would."[14] "Endings and beginnings" are the rhythm of life, rhythm of seasons, and the circle of life in this earth. As people committed to the church and to our role in the church, we are also committed to an intentional and healthy approach to this ebb and flow. One musician advises:

> Find a trusted friend to tell you that you will survive this and come out better in the long run! Someone did that for me about three months after I left the church and by then I was ready to hear it. That was probably the hardest part of it. Your head tells you (hopefully) "Get out with

> dignity," but the reality of not having the self-defined role of "church musician" means that you have to relearn who you are in your worship life. There is also the pain of learning to simply attend church and not be leading music. It is a good thing to learn to do in reality, but it is hard to sit back and not evaluate, to learn to worship again. I think that is part of the healing as well.[15]

Yes, we will want to give ourselves time to adjust. It may be painful, but it will be worth the effort to work at making this transition a productive benefit to our well-being. Specifically,

- Rejoice in all the good you did, the wonderful ministry you had, and the great people with whom you shared your ministry. If there are things you wish you had done differently, move them to the margins of your thoughts, for the moment anyway.
- Focus on the future, the chance to take a breath before moving on, the chance to redirect yourself personally or professionally, or the exciting opportunities that await you.
- Making the transition as positive as you can will make you feel better and will also help those who are regretting your departure. Your attitude will signal the way others approach the transition.
- Receive the affirmation that comes your way with gratitude and joy; you have made a difference in the lives of many people, and they will want to show their appreciation.
- Accept that the transition won't be perfect. Something will get missed, bungled, or translated in the wrong way. Expect there will be days you regret having left, even if the next position is an exciting one. It's hard to leave a place you have loved; feeling sad is understandable. Of course, you will feel down about it. But, it would be more of a shame if you didn't.
- Turn to others for support. Seek out friends who have been through this, or simply friends who can offer love and support. Meet them for lunch or coffee at least once a week.
- Go deeper by connecting with a group at a church or community organization that acts as support to people in job transition.
- Explore spiritual direction or counseling.
- Write in a journal.

- Take care of yourself during the time of transition. Exercise, try yoga or meditation. Do something you've been meaning to do when you had the time: read a book in that two-foot stack on the coffee table, digitize and label those old slides stored in the family room, take a cooking class or a course on archaeology at a local community college.

Beginning Anew

It is time to come to grips with reality. You have changed and the world has changed since you last applied for a job. Even if only a few years have passed, there are at least three key factors to consider:

- The recent economic collapse has forced churches to change the way they operate and has limited the financial support they have available for salaries and programs.
- Church attendance is more mercurial, denominational loyalty is less strong, and many churches are simply having a tough time attracting and retaining members.
- Alternative worship styles and expanded musical styles make new demands on musicians that should be considered before you even tackle the job market.

"To begin a new job," explains Bridges, "is to encounter the same kinds of difficulties that one finds in the beginning of a new relationship. There is a period of adjustment in each case, though 'adjustment' is a misleading mechanistic concept. It suggests that you need to fiddle with the dials and reset the switches to adapt yourself to the new situation. The trouble with this view is that, although there are difficult changes to be made as one gets used to a new situation, the difficulty comes not from these changes but from the larger process of letting go of the person you used to be and then finding the new person you have become in the new situation."[16]

First, take a personal inventory:

- Identify your strongest skills. What do you do best?
- Identify managerial and administrative as well as musical skills
- List the characteristics you value: What do you want in this position? What do you want that you didn't have in your former job?

- Look at yourself honestly. Are there habits or attitudes that might have held you back in a previous job? Might they have prevented your achieving the success you had the talent to achieve?
- Be willing to work at the areas that need to be changed.
- Broaden your skills to meet the demands of the current market. Churches may be looking for people with skills that you don't currently have. If you don't improvise well, can't play off a lead sheet, want to feel more confident in your vocal techniques or conducting skills, or work with praise bands and sound technicians, take some lessons or get some coaching and work to add these to your repertoire of skills.
- Update your resume and write a compelling (and rigorously proofread) cover letter. Seek help from a job counseling service or a friend.
- Network by contacting colleagues and friends about job openings.
- Network using social media to share news of your availability and the kind of work you hope to find.
- If your knowledge of technology is sketchy, remedy that.
- Make sure your appearance is professional and that you look like the kind of person the church will feel lucky to hire.
- Take a personality inventory (Myers-Briggs or another one) so that, if asked, you will be able to share your "type" with the committee. They may already know the types of other staff members, and many churches want to ensure that they are hiring people who have a good chance of working together well.[17] It's been noted that the predominant types for clergy are ENFJ, ESFJ and ENFP—how does your type work with those?
- If you hear about a position that is open, check with a trusted colleague or two before applying. You need to know as much about it as possible, including reasons why previous musicians have left. Colleagues will want to remain professional and keep confidences, but ask gently and tell them why you want to know. There is always someone who will know something about the situation and be able to advise you.
- Talk to musicians and other staff members who are no longer on staff but who worked at the church with the same clergy, if you can. Or talk to musicians who may have worked with them at another church. In all of these contacts you will want to promise confidentiality and keep it.

- Consider coaching on interviewing skills, especially if you haven't done an interview recently. And you will want to practice ahead of time.
- Look carefully at any potential position. Don't jump at the first offer unless you are truly going to lose your house or starve if you don't take it.
- Make sure the position is what you are really looking for or at least one in which you have the hope of finding fulfillment.
- Check the church's website. What ministries does it have? How is the vision and mission described? Where is the music program? Is it buried in the web site or does it appear up front?

Having identified a church you might consider, do your homework:

- Attend several services at the church to get a true sense of the congregation, its worship style, and the way music fits into its services. Is the congregation friendly? Does it sing enthusiastically? Does the music seem to matter? How is the preaching? Is there a sense of cohesion in the congregation? It has been said that congregational health can be measured in two ways: the way the congregation sings and the way they pass the peace. Do the members sit far apart and barely greet one another at the passing of the peace or at the end of the service?
- Consider attending a small group such as a Bible study or one that makes sandwiches for the homeless on Saturday mornings.
- Educate yourself on the culture of the church, its values, its mission, its spirituality. It is one thing to see oneself as being successful in the new position (a necessary step to becoming successful), but first you want a real sense that you will be working with people who will help you achieve that success.
- Try to get a sense of the way people communicate with each other. Step aside and watch as the clergy greet people at the end of the service. Is there a genuine sense of caring, or is it a perfunctory greeting? Again, listen to the after-service conversation. Do members of the congregation seem to hold each other in genuine affection?
- As part of the interview process, ask to see the music library, review past worship bulletins and newsletters, inquire as to qualities that have been valued about previous music programs, ask about changes they would like to see made in the future, and note whether the changes they mention are small or large. Do you have a sense that the worship and personnel committees will partner with you in these changes? Will they expect you to take the initiative?

- Inquire as to what support is available to the music program. Is planning time with senior clergy available? Is there an adequate budget for the program the church leadership envisions? What about rehearsal space and instruments? Is there volunteer support (for example, parents to assist with children's choirs)? These questions—and their answers—will help you discern whether or not the church values the program. Failure to value a program is one of the principal reasons musicians leave a church, so look carefully.

If this is still a position of interest, ask to see a complete job description and the proposed contract, one that lists specifically what the church expects. Read these documents carefully for what is included, but more important, for what is not.

Be prepared to help the church identify the amount of time it expects from the musician based on the administrative, musical, and worship responsibilities it requires. The American Guild of Organists has a set of model contract provisions and a very helpful template to guide congregations to a realistic understanding of the church musician's tasks, many of which are often taken for granted. Insisting that responsibilities be clarified in writing beforehand will save untold angst later on.

Pay particular attention to the gray areas where some tasks might be done by more than one person. For example, who picks the hymns: the clergy, the musician, a worship team, or the staff? As previously discussed, this can be a point of acute tension. Know what the church's practice is. Less important, but with similar potential for confusion, is the question of bulletin preparation. At some churches, a church secretary or administrative assistant performs this clerical function; at others, the service leaflet is prepared by the clergy or the musician. It is important to know these and other expectations from the very beginning.

In addition, you'll want to be clear on these questions:

- How will you be evaluated, by whom, when, and on what criteria?
- If differences arise, how are they resolved? Is mediation offered?
- What is the chain of command? How does the musician relate to senior clergy and to the personnel committee?
- Compensation questions: When are staff paid? How are raises handled? What are the benefits? Is health insurance provided? Are there retirement benefits? Are there continuing education funds? Is there time off for vacation and for continuing education events? If not used, can vacation and sick leave be carried over from one year to the next?

- Who receives requests for purchasing music and other items for the music program? Do you need approval before ordering such items?
- Who arranges for a substitute when the resident organist cannot be there for a service?
- If the organist plays for weddings and funerals, who establishes the fee?
- If the organist does not play for weddings and funerals, who does, and who on the church staff makes those arrangements?
- Will the salary be adjusted if services or choirs are added?
- If you wish to teach organ students, will the church instrument be available? Will your students be able to practice at the church and will there be a charge for practice time?

Finally, obvious as they may seem, here are some subjects that you might use to start developing the healthy relationship you hope to have with your colleague(s) in ministry. You're not a reporter, and this isn't an investigation, but if you need some ideas for breaking the ice, you might ask:

- What do you most like to do in your spare time?
- Are you into sports? What teams to do you follow?
- What is your favorite holiday?
- Who is your favorite childhood friend? Are you still in touch? What did you do together that was fun?
- What's the last book you read that you loved?

You might get more worship/music specific with low-intensity points like these.

- I was drawn to this (music/pastoral) ministry because ...
- These are my favorite hymns ... because ...
- My favorite season of the church year is ... because ...
- My favorite part of the church building i ... because ...
- I prepare for Sunday services by doing ...
- To make sure the skills I'll need are always "on" I ...
- The book on music/worship that I have found most helpful is ...

It's just like dating—this business of looking at a job listing, deciding whether to apply, accepting the vulnerability of interviewing, and then considering the position. Once in the new position, it can take weeks or months to know and grow to trust each other. For you and your new colleagues, thus begin your first steps down the path of figuring out how to work together most productively and creatively.

Notes

1. Cheryl Duerr, The Concord Coaching Company, e-mail to author, January 5, 2012.
2. Maxwell, *The 17 Essential Qualities*, 122.
3. [Name withheld], e-mail to author, September 1, 2011.
4. [Name withheld], e-mail to author, August 15, 2009.
5. Debi Tyree, e-mail to author, September 9, 2011.
6. William Bridges, *Transitions: Making Sense of Life's Changes,* Cambridge, MA: Perseus Books, 1980, 9.
7. *Ibid.,* 13.
8. *Ibid.,* 96.
9. *Ibid.,* 100.
10. *Ibid.*
11. *Ibid.,* 101-102.
12. *Ibid.,* 103–104.
13. *Ibid.,* 110.
14. Bridges, 150.
15. Debi Tyree, e-mail to author, September 8, 2011.
16. Bridges, 74–75.
17. Cheryl Duerr, e-mail to author, January 5, 2012.

10
Reflections on Being a Church Musician

When the prophetic and proclaiming Word (preaching) can link up with the prophetic and proclaiming song, there's nothing like it. Being a church musician is a great profession, a great calling. It has its own form of tenure: love God, love the people, and love and respect those who are called to serve alongside us.

—David Cherwien

I asked colleagues around the country to reflect on their calling, their careers, and clergy with whom they had worked, and I am grateful for the mirrors they have held up to their professional lives as evidenced by the following reflections.

Philip Brunelle
Organist-Choirmaster
Plymouth Congregational Church, Minneapolis, Minnesota
Artistic Director and Founder, VocalEssence

At age fifteen I began my career as a church organist, adding the duties of choir director a few years later. Of course, with my father being a minister I was a regular every Sunday morning and evening as well as Wednesday prayer meetings; I was a boy soprano soloist starting at age three and accompanist for services and meetings starting in junior high. My first organ position was at a small suburban Covenant church, moving to a large Covenant church two years later, then at age twenty-one to a Lutheran church and at age twenty-five to Plymouth Congregational Church where I am now in my forty-third year. I am the third organist-choirmaster at Plymouth Church since 1900!

Plymouth Church is well-known as a theologically liberal bastion in Minneapolis, as it has been since its founding in 1856. Its membership of two thousand is a melting pot of congregants who, for the most part, are people formerly associated with some other denomination...or none at all. It is a church that embraces Progressive Christianity and is also a church with a long-standing embrace of the arts, which it encourages as a source of religious nourishment. During my time at Plymouth there have been three senior ministers, each one very different from the other, as well as a host of associate ministers.

So, how does a church musician maintain a healthy, collegial relationship with clergy? First of all, I must say that my years at Plymouth Church have been wonderful. I have heard stories from my colleagues about difficulties in clergy relationships—and I have had none of that! I suspect that one of the reasons is my belief that I am serving at the behest of the minister and congregation. When I arrived at Plymouth Church, the senior minister at the time assumed that I would join the church. I informed him that I would not—*but* that I would tithe to Plymouth.

I have spent my life in church work knowing that the senior minister has the final say—not the organist. I do not view the relationship between the two of us as fifty-fifty, but rather ninety-ten. I must be willing to go ninety percent of the way in the relationship as necessary to maintain a healthy partnership.

The balance of music in worship is a delicate one, and I am very conscious about its role and place in the service. With the diversity of background in any congregation and with the various alluring styles of music available in today's world, it has been a challenge to maintain a service with integrity, with music that enhances the worship for the day. But it has worked and Plymouth continues to grow...singing hymn verses unaccompanied, hearing anthems from around the globe, and celebrating the rich heritage that sacred music has to offer.

What does it come down to? Communication—keeping the lines open. Of course, there have been strains—but nothing that could not be remedied where trust and communication exist. When that happens, then the preaching and the music share a wonderful balance and the results each Sunday are blessed.

David Cherwien
Artistic Director, National Lutheran Choir
Cantor, Mount Olive Lutheran Church, Minneapolis, Minnesota

As a college student preparing to be a high-school choir teacher, I played in a rock band five nights a week. I had played piano since kindergarten and organ since seventh grade. While I enjoyed that, I didn't find the heart of what I felt called to be until attending a Paul Manz hymn festival. In that experience I saw all of my skills and experiences brought together. Was I choir director? Organist? Teacher? Improvising rock musician? None of the above. I was to be a "congregation player" putting all of those skills together to draw people of God together in song as one voice. No easy task.

As I reflect on the eight faith communities I have served, these congregations were like our four family cats: all cats, but each one dramatically different. Each community of faith had its own personality, interests, and responses. Serving these people effectively demanded three things: knowing them, loving them, and knowing how to be the prophet in their midst by challenging them to grow, to sing better, and to experience and share God in new and deeper ways. Being prophetic also includes a constant effort to keep people connected to their own past journey and memory as a community, and with the past journey and memory of all of God's people.

When congregations respond in song, there's nothing like it. Corporate singing is such a miracle in our time. We have become either spectators or listeners. It is so extremely rare to join in song with others in public that it is astonishing when it happens. It has been my hope, prayer, and goal to create a judgment-free atmosphere that empowers freedom and authenticity to sing—to know we have left the world of self and stepped into something far greater.

This focus has driven my working relationships with pastors. Our focus has been: God, the people and their connection to God and each other, and how we serve both of those as staff. It can be hard work to stay focused on the people and their connection to God and each other, and not get distracted by turf issues between pastor and musician. The hard but necessary work for the musician is putting oneself in the pastor's shoes. Often pastors need to be on top of things in order to feel they are doing their job. The question becomes: Can I still do what I need to do on behalf of the people and help the pastor have a sense of being in control? It has been challenging, creative, and at times subversive.

I've learned that pastor-musician relationships are also like our cats: no two collegial relationships have been the same. What has consistently been important is mutual respect. I have found that keeping God and the people first in mind tends to resolve turf issues appropriately.

I have learned that when the prophetic and proclaiming Word (preaching) can link up with the prophetic and proclaiming song, there's nothing like it. People notice and are energized. This is where the energy needs to be spent.

Being a church musician is a great profession, a great calling. It has its own form of tenure: love God, love the people, and love and respect those who are called to serve alongside us.

Jason Kissel
Director of Music and Organist
First and Franklin Presbyterian Church, Baltimore Maryland

A teacher instilled in our undergraduate organ studio how crucial it is for church musicians to embody three roles in one—minister, educator, and musician, in that order. Since that time, I have often reminded myself of this "Holy Trinity," particularly during times I have felt the need to regain perspective on my work.

I think there are musicians who happen to work in churches, and then there are church musicians—those for whom working collegially in order to administer, plan, and lead in the dynamic worship of God is the response to a significant, and perhaps, lifelong calling. When I reflect on my position as director of music and organist of a Baltimore congregation for the past decade, the underlying success of my work results from the relationships I have cultivated and the mutual trust and support I have established with choir members and congregants. A church musician must have a genuine interest in others and be able to relate to those with whom they work. The pastoral care a church musician provides can assume many forms—from providing a listening ear to a choir member who is facing a life struggle to the manner in which we register and accompany hymns for congregational singing. It is also important to mention the necessity of modeling the religious and caring nature of the church in all our encounters, whether in meetings, rehearsals, or written communication.

The educational and musical aspects of the "Trinity" might seem obvious but, apart from achieving the appropriate technical mastery for the job at hand, I believe the church musician has the responsibility of educating the community in scriptural rhetoric as it pertains to the music selected for worship. I think congregants and ensembles best experience or present a piece of music when they have knowledge not only of its musical origin but also its message for their own lives of faith. Another important part of a church musician's job as educator is continually to seek ways of building community—community within the church that includes ensembles and committees, community that bridges the music program with other churches and institutions, and community that invites people to experience and embrace music and worship of other cultures.

For a fine church musician, the roles of minister, educator, and musician work together to form a whole. To me, being a church musician means focusing the use of my talent to foster seamless, Christ- or God-centered worship. Corporate worship, the central and most important act of any congregation, cannot emerge when the focus is placed upon an individual person. Just as we expect that clergy will inspire and guide our thoughts to that which is holy, church musicians must also strive to use their skills and artistry to help others discover a "more profound Alleluia!"

Julie Vidrick Evans
Director of Music
Chevy Chase Presbyterian Church, Chevy Chase, Maryland

Relationships between clergy and musicians can be as varied and intense as relationships between any two people. There can be an intimate collegial sharing—a working together that can produce a sublime spiritual experience for the congregation, or the relationship can be fraught with tension, misunderstanding, and distrust.

Like all human relationships, the best clergy-musician relationships are built on trust, respect, confidence in one another's skills, and a shared vision. There is another complication. In most churches, the musician is a subordinate to the clergy. This means that, when things turn bad, it is generally the musician who has to leave. If you are in that situation, it is wisest to get out quickly.

A good clergy-musician relationship, like a good marriage, requires commitment and hard work. You must constantly seek greater communication and mutual understanding. As a musician, your job is to provide artistic and responsive support for the service and to illuminate the message. You cannot do this if you and the clergy do not totally understand one another. You don't have to agree with or even believe the same things the pastor does, although it might help. None of this is possible without trust and confidence. To say that I trust my superior or my subordinate means that I believe that he or she shares my values and intentions and will do the right thing. To say that I have confidence in that person is to say that I believe they are capable of doing what needs to be done, that they are competent. If either is lacking, then the relationship is not functional.

A pastor has to trust that the musician shares the vision and will work to realize that vision and not have a separate agenda. The musician has to trust that the pastor is a person of God, who will listen to—and value—the musician's advice. Mutual trust is key.

Similarly, the pastor has to have confidence that the musician has the requisite musical skills and judgment. The musician has to have the confidence that the pastor understands the congregation and the vision and has the requisite pastoral skills and intent.

It is important to remember that the relationship between pastor and musician is a relationship between leaders. So, one has to take into account different leadership styles. If the leadership styles are very different, then levels of trust and confidence will need to be even more aligned.

My personal experience has put me in several types of partnerships. My most satisfying work relationship has been in a situation where the clergyman was a leader who had strong vision and communicated that to his staff. He was supportive, trusting and trustworthy, and took great delight in designing services that relied on the musician's education and skill each week. Participating in discussions about choosing hymns to illuminate the message, and the appropriate placement of hymns and anthems was a great joy for me. My preference is not to work in a vacuum in planning corporate worship. My least satisfying relationship was one that eroded over time because I had little trust that the pastor would carry out things we agreed on, after promising to do so. It is my opinion that if you don't have mutual trust and confidence in your pastor, you need to search for another position.

Karen A. Rich
Church musician
Tulsa, Oklahoma

The best clergy-musician relationship I have experienced in forty years as a church musician was based on three simple components: communication, commitment, and compassion.

Communication. You expect clergypersons to be good speakers, although some are disappointing in that regard. My clergyman was an excellent speaker, but his ability to listen was exceptional. I never heard him interrupt anyone who was speaking, and I often heard him use the active-listener phrase, "What I hear you saying is ..." Staff meetings were fun—a time for each person to share what was going on in our own lives, in our areas of responsibility at the church, and in the church as a whole. No detail was too small, no idea was too large to escape his attention: if it was important to us, it was important to him.

He knew that the church was proud of its history of good music and was always complimentary and supportive. The success of the music program did not threaten him—he actively looked for ways to highlight the skills of the volunteers and leadership who made it possible. It was a pleasure working with someone who trusted my judgment, knowledge, and skill enough to allow me such great freedom. Because we planned far enough in advance, it wasn't unusual for a reference to a choral anthem or hymn being sung to appear in the sermon. He cared enough about the service as a whole to study the music and see how it fit in with the lectionary readings. We met every week to talk about the service. He knew that if he wanted to use a different hymn, or go a different direction with his sermon, we could talk about it. He would never make an arbitrary change. I respected his knowledge, and he respected mine.

Commitment. His involvement and interest in the church were evident from his first days there. He made a point of learning names and relationships of members. He studied the history of the church and learned everything he could about the historic building. He sought the advice of elderly members and listened for hours to their stories of "the way it used to be." He never expected anyone to do anything that he would not do. We were always encouraged to involve as many people in the church as we could. We helped each other in identifying potential recruits and developing individual talents. We wanted to do our very best, and the church benefitted from the group camaraderie and creativity.

Compassion. He never forgot an important event in a church member's life—birthday, anniversary, death. His date book was full of the information that he gleaned from talking to staff and church members. The phone call, or the card, or the email quietly went to the recipient. The hospital visits, the visits to homebound members, the visits to nursing homes—all were important to him. He was an excellent counselor, partly because of his great listening skills, and partly because you knew that anything you told him would be kept in absolute confidence. The church had a significant number of elderly members, and he counseled many families who were at a loss when it came to planning a funeral or memorial service. So, at his instigation, we started talking to groups within the church, helping them plan services for themselves or loved ones.

I am so grateful for the almost ten years that we worked together, the happiest and most productive time of my professional career.

Russell Miller
Minister of Music and Worship
First United Methodist Church, Boerne, Texas

Reflecting on over twenty-five years as a church musician, I have come to understand, at least to some degree, the depth of meaning associated with being a church musician. For some, a church musician's job is seen as little more than rehearsing during the week to prepare music for Sunday worship. Yet that barely skims the surface. Underlying that weekly routine for me is the ministry of relationship: relationship with God and relationship with others. The medium of music gives me an avenue to meet God that is more intense and more personal than words alone can offer, and I am so very grateful to have been given access to that gift! That gift then allows me to use music and the other creative arts in worship to help others also deepen their relationship with God. But unless I am also in relationship with those in my congregation, those efforts in worship are limited in their effectiveness. When those in my choirs and congregation know me not only as a musician, but as a committed disciple of Christ, as a fellow traveler who struggles with the hard questions, as a tither, as one who is willing to step outside the walls of the church to be in ministry with the poor and the downtrodden, and as someone who authentically cares for them, then—and only then—does the musician's gift truly bear fruit.

Michael Bedford
Organist-Choirmaster, Composer-in-Residence
St. John's Episcopal Church, Tulsa, Oklahoma

I have served St. John's Episcopal Church in Tulsa, Oklahoma for twenty-one years now, and about six years ago the church hired a new rector. This can be a stressful time as both new and current staff members strive to find exactly where they and their various programs fit into the new scheme of things.

I could not have been more pleased with the way our new rector integrated himself into an already successful situation. He began his tenure in a congenial and supportive manner, lifting up each staff member and praising them for the fine work they were doing. Not only did he wait an entire year before making any major changes to the existing structure of services and programming, but he also shared each new idea he had with the person whose program was affected. Before implementing any new plan, he asked the advice of all involved and listened to all questions and concerns. There were no changes until everyone was comfortable with them. The general approach was that if the new idea did not work, then we would go back to the original concept.

From his first day among us, our rector has supported every aspect of the music program. Consequently, when he approached the other clergy and me about the possibility of a late afternoon alternative worship service on Sundays, I entered into the discussion with a completely open mind. I found myself wanting to support him in a venture that was near and dear to his heart. As a classically-trained musician, the more contemporary music for this service was a bit out of my realm. Since I was not familiar with these musical resources, we decided that our new young curate could be of help. He knows many sources from which to draw for music, plays the guitar beautifully, and has a lovely singing voice. With him and another young parishioner on guitars and me on keyboard, we have a basic music team. Our curate plans the music, and the three of us rehearse once a week in order to prepare for the service.

Through broadening my perspective on liturgical music, I have opened a whole new door in my worship life. At sixty-two years of age, I have learned a valuable lesson from this experience. I now know that sometimes our hearts are just too full for one means of musical expression. I would not trade my classical background or our more traditional Sunday morning worship for anything, but I have discovered a whole new means of musical expression that reaches a little deeper into my soul and touches on aspects of the Holy that up to now have never been tapped.

The proverbial concept that "an old dog can learn new tricks" has never been more apparent to me than it is now. This I have learned from a man who is twenty years my junior, but who came to our church family with an air of congeniality and respect that has endeared him to staff and congregation alike. I feel that over the past six years our rector and I have grown both in our spiritual lives and in the way we respect and revere each other. For me this kind of mutual support and sharing are what spell success for any church.

C. Milton Rodgers III
Minister of Music and Organist
Grace United Methodist Church, Manassas, Virginia

Ministers of music have some of the most privileged duties in the world. We are tasked with caring for people and then providing ways that our parishioners can open their souls to experience God here on earth. Our means of creating that communication between the parishioner and God is through the music, which God created in the first place.

I have always loved the church, I have always loved music, and I have known since I was ten years old that I wanted to be a minister of music. This calling by God took everything to a higher level. While at Westminster Choir College, I learned the difference between being a "director of music" and a "minister of music." For some of my colleagues, church music was simply about having a choir to perform music they wanted to direct, but for me it was different. I thought of my choirs as consisting of living, loving beings who needed to be nurtured. I learned that when they realized I really cared about them as human beings, they would put forth their very best efforts for me and for God.

I became a diaconal minister in the United Methodist Church and was thrilled when the General Conference of the church acknowledged that those of us who were called to music ministry could go through the steps of becoming deacons or ordained clergy. The deacon is called to connect the church to the world and the world to the church. Music is the perfect means for this. As a deacon, I am required every year to report on who I have helped to enable these connections.

I will never forget my ordination in 2001 by Bishop Joe Pennel. In tears, he charged us that we would be with people at the most important parts of their lives—their birth, their marriage, and their death. I take that to heart every day. It is our job as ministers of music to make people aware that God is with them through every event in life. God provides the words and the music for all of the passages of life.

In seminary I learned that the Kingdom of God has already happened and yet will still come to be. We experience this truth all the time in church music. I love to go to handbell festivals and events sponsored by the American Choral Directors Association and American Guild of Organists, where I can be fed musically with almost perfect performances. I can then take these performances back to the church with me and give the choirs the vision of perfection that God wants. Mistakes may happen and that is okay as long as we have done our very best for God. Perfection is a part of that Kingdom which "will still come to be."

Alice Mikolajewski
Minister of Music and Liturgy
The Basilica of St. Paul, Daytona Beach, Florida

When I arrived at the Basilica, I came with a very strong musical background, but was new to liturgical planning, which also is a large part of this job. My title is Minister of Music and Liturgy. Although I have a strong Catholic background, there was much to learn.

Fr. Timothy Daly is the pastor here at the Basilica of St. Paul. At the time of my audition and interview, the committee had asked Fr. Tim directly, "How do you think your work relationship will be with Alice?" The committee understood the importance of that relationship since this position puts me working very closely with him.

Fr. Tim immediately scheduled weekly meetings with me where we went through the liturgy in detail. He taught me about the planning and details that needed to be addressed each week. We went through the Sacramentary as well as numerous additional materials. Both he and our seminarian at that time gave me books and lots of advice when needed. It was most comforting to know that if I did have a question, Fr. Tim was never more than a phone call or text away. Because he has so many various duties in the community, he is not always easily accessible at the church. Despite this, he always responds promptly.

We soon discovered that we thought alike in many ways. This certainly made our working relationship run smoother. We were often thinking of making similar or the same changes and adjustments in our efforts for all to run smoothly. I learned very quickly and worked hard to fulfill my responsibilities. I never felt as though he was hovering over me. He would introduce materials for specific events and occasions, and then would let me take care of everything. I sometimes would go to him so that he could double check my work (especially when it was a complicated mass with extraordinary music and text), and he would make any necessary changes.

Knowing that he trusted my judgment and had confidence in the work I presented gave me the strength to not be timid. He does not hesitate, though, to express himself if something needs changing or doesn't work. Discussion is always welcomed and encouraged when there are issues to address. He never makes me feel inadequate, and he is not one to place blame. He also is not shy to admit when he has erred as well. He always reminds me of how grateful he is to have me here and appreciative of my work. He is wonderful at recognizing when I go above and beyond the job description. I never feel as though I am taken for granted. When new ideas arise, all of us here have the freedom to explore them. Not everything works all the time, but at least we have the opportunity to try them.

I am very lucky to be in a situation where I can express myself and be heard. I am also most fortunate to be in a position where there is mutual respect for the other person, and certainly an appreciation for the skills they bring to the church.

Robert E. Young
Director of Music Ministries
Asbury Church, Salisbury, Maryland

After a new pastor was called to the Lutheran church I was serving, it was clear that the music program there would be short-lived. I left, and moved to a small, coastal community. Within two weeks, a priestly type man was knocking at the door. "Hello, I understand you have just moved here and are a professional church musician. Could I make an appointment to speak with you?" This ultimately led to my being in front of twelve not-so-good singers, an Episcopal congregation of about eighty in a church that would seat about 180, and my fingers on an old Möller organ. There was no piano in the sanctuary, just a spinet in the choir room. What *was* I doing?

I remember my first Sunday with this parish and the preparation that preceded it. I was asked by the rector to play through everything with him for that first worship service. He insisted on doing the registration, telling me when and where to push pistons, and how tempos were to be established and maintained. I gently looked this man in the eyes and said, "My friend, I have been doing this for forty years, professionally, and I assure you, I am capable of registering, playing, and leading worship effectively." He was very nice, said thank you, got off the organ bench, and went to his office.

But I soon learned not to ask for anything from this rector. To ask for anything, even a particular hymn, would result in a speech about who was in charge and guarantee that whatever I asked for would never again be discussed. The first time I heard the words, "If you do not obey, I will do with you as I do with my wife," they flew over my head. I had never before been anywhere near such an experience, and it took two more hearings of those words before I realized what was going on, and how I had allowed myself to be in a position of abuse. Eventually, for my own mental health, I had to leave, after almost ten years. Parishioners could not understand, since both the rector and I had kept all the mess behind the scenes.

Soon, I was approached by an AGO member, working at some big Methodist church about an hour south, who told me he wanted me to play at his church for three months. He had been trying to take a sabbatical for five years, before retirement, never successful at arranging for another organist to be on board for the three-month period of time needed for the sabbatical. I accepted on the condition that all I had do was show up on Thursday to direct adult choir rehearsals and play two Sunday services only. Before beginning my three-month tenure on the first of January, I went to a worship service on the Sunday before Christmas to get the lay of the land. I missed the Episcopal liturgy, but the service was dignified, in good taste, with music very well-executed and in a worshipful manner. I was excited! The next three months were filled with wonderful times with this choir. The main attraction for me during these three months was the words from the preaching pastor. He knew nothing about me and had no idea who was sitting behind him at the organ and directing this choir. I let this pastor know, many times, how important his words were to me. My three-month tenure ended and I departed.

Three years later, my phone rang. It was this same pastor from the sabbatical: "Our director of music is retiring, and we would like to talk with you about coming to work with us." It has been eight years so far—and the fulfillment of many dreams. All that I endured, I believe, was for me to learn to be able to move forward successfully and to help others in similar situations via my music and my presence. I know there are many places where pastors and musicians cannot understand each other. We need to work on this, as pastors and musicians. We each have so much to offer.

Name withheld
Organist and Choirmaster
Presbyterian Church

In my opinion, the clergy-musician relationship centers on power. Music is sometimes a more powerful force than speech in affecting an immediate change in how people feel. That ability to inspire people in just a few minutes can be seen as a real threat to a less-than-confident cleric. Further, texts we learn through music stick with us longer than hearing words alone.

On the other hand, imagine the synergy of a relationship where thoughtful, scholarly, theological concepts are blended with and supported by sensitive musical choices—a liturgy that incorporates the best of what each brings to the table. If only we musicians and clergy didn't so frequently live in distrust of one another.

I believe most of us, when confronted with a real or perceived threat, respond in ways to protect ourselves. In a conflicted relationship, without intervention, our behavior can lead to isolation and, more often than not, the break-up of a relationship. Both parties lose.

Example: a newly-assigned clergyperson arrives with an agenda to clear out the old staff and build a new one. I was one of nine full-time staffers when a new senior minister was called; a year later, I was the only one left. During the next six years, I saw an additional twenty staff come and go. In some cases, the firings were justified, but could have been avoided had the pastor and search committee done their due diligence to make sure the candidate could really do the job in the first place. I cannot remember one person who left—or was encouraged to leave—because they felt called to a new place. It was a typical situation of being forced out.

The irony in this situation is that during those seven years, everything looked rosy: the congregation grew, contributions increased, we built a marvelous new nave with a magnificent organ. There were lots of good times and happy achievements. But staffers rarely knew when they had fallen out of favor until it was too late. The pastor avoided conflict, and when he had finally had enough (from his perspective), he'd call a staffer in and tell them things just weren't working out. When I left to go to another church, the pastor was actually surprised when I told him I had accepted a new position. But, because of the working situation at that church, I had been looking in earnest for most of the seven years!

The most painful situation—and the one that I felt bordered on unethical behavior—was at a church where I worked for six years. Although I asked repeatedly during my tenure there, I never had one bona fide performance review, either with the pastor or worship committee. In the two times I was "evaluated," questionnaires were handed out—in one case to the choir, in another to the worship committee. Both came back with favorable comments. Never during the six years did I feel listened to by the worship committee when I shared my vision and what I needed to do my job effectively.

When the pastor left for another church and the interim came, I discovered that I had been "shielded" from a few very influential choir members who weren't getting to sing enough of the music they wanted to do. And I was accused of making choir too hard, if you call insisting on regular attendance, good diction, and accurate intonation a distasteful thing. Similarly, the chair of the personnel committee discovered that I had been kept in the dark for most of the time I had been there. However, at that point it was too late to do anything to resolve the conflict. The interim took us through a Presbyterian-style process of gathering information from the various groups before the personnel committee handed down their decision that they believed we had gotten to a place where my ability to succeed there was compromised, and I was given two months' severance pay.

Alvin D. (Ted) Gustin
Organist
First Church of Christ Scientist, Alexandria, Virginia and
Beth El Hebrew Congregation, Alexandria, Virginia

After serving for almost forty years as organist-choirmaster at a prominent, nationally known Episcopal church, I was shocked to see, while browsing on the church's website, that my job would be open and available in a matter of weeks. This was news to me!! Shocking news! In fact, a search committee was already in place to start announcing and eventually selecting the right person to replace me. I couldn't believe it!

I was instructed to tell members of the congregation and the choirs that I was "retiring" from my position, which was definitely not true. I loved my job, the people, and the beautiful church itself. I wasn't going to lie about anything, no matter how much easier it would be for the rector. The people were not happy with the news. I was forced to tell the congregation five months early that I would be leaving my position on a certain date. I refused to say I was resigning or retiring, but leaving. I would not lie! One lady in the congregation with terminal cancer said to me: "You better not leave this church! I want you to play for my funeral!" I did end up playing for her funeral but at the anger of the rector, who yelled out to me, "You sabotaged me!" Members of the family of the deceased had taken to the vestry their demand that I play for the family funeral. The senior warden agreed that I would play, after discussing it with the vestry. Everybody who attended the funeral service reception was delighted that I had played for the service. The rector asked me to hand in my keys after the funeral and reception, which I graciously did.

I felt I had lost almost all my dear friends after working with and for them most of my adult life. That job was the love of my life—my life's dream, soon to be gone.

The next shock was to learn that my successor would receive a salary nearly three times what I had been paid after forty years of service. Upon inquiry, I was told I had been there so long that they never really had any reason to even inquire as to what organist-choirmasters should be making—with *two* Bachelor's degrees and a master's degree in church music. "We must have had our heads buried in the sand like ostriches," they admitted. "We just didn't know what organist–choirmasters were supposed to be earning." Some excuse! Oh, by the way, I really worked there *full* time for part-time pay! But I *loved* every minute of it! I survived it all and have moved on. What choice did I have?

Sarah Hawbecker
Organist and Director of Music for Children and Youth
Lutheran Church of the Redeemer, Atlanta, Georgia

For me, being a church musician is my life; it is part of who I am. If our purpose in life is to become who God created us to be, then I believe that I am definitely on that path. I am a musician who has answered the call to use my gifts in a specific place. It has not always been an easy call; sometimes, it has felt like more of a shove or a magnetic pull than an invitation.

I have been in my current full-time position for over sixteen years, serving a large parish that has been through its own highs and lows. In this position, I have worked with nine different musical colleagues (both paid and volunteer staff), numerous associate pastors and other program staff, and most significantly, three different senior pastors plus two interim senior pastors. Through the years, I have experienced varying styles and degrees of teamwork.

In my opinion, the most important characteristic of a healthy clergy and musician relationship is mutual respect. Mutual respect allows us to recognize each other's gifts and call, enables us to listen, and builds the foundation of the partnership that supports us even when we disagree. If two people cannot communicate with each other, are dishonest with each other, or cannot work through differences, the relationship starts to crumble. The church is the body of Christ. When one relationship is not working well, especially one that involves the most visible and "up front" people during a worship service, it affects the whole body, the whole family.

I wonder whether situations might improve if there were more schools in which pastors and musicians could study and live together. The current culture is that we go our separate ways. The best musicians go to music conservatories to study and get little, if any, theological training. Seminarians often receive very little musical training. It can't be that much of a surprise, then, that when we are thrown together to work, feelings of competitiveness, wariness, and distrust emerge.

Sadly, the church as an institution is not an easy place in which to work. Having grown up as a "preacher's kid" and having worked in the church full time as an adult, I feel like I've seen it all. So why do I still do it? It's how I live my life to God. If I weren't making music, it would feel as if I had lost a limb, or even my soul. Making music in the church, and most important, teaching others to make music and enabling those gathered to worship to give themselves to God through their song, is to fulfill my call. When this is recognized by my pastor, I feel incredibly supported, and it makes a huge difference in my work.

Although there are musicians for whom their Sunday morning job is just another gig, it certainly is not the case for me and for countless others. When I play the organ or conduct an ensemble for a Sunday service, wedding, or funeral, I try to remember that the music may speak to someone in a profound way. What may be routine for me as a musician could possibly affect the listener very deeply. I recognize this possibility and take the responsibility seriously. If I were to think that church music didn't matter, I would have to stop doing it. When musicians and clergy are partners in allowing the Spirit to be at work in worship in this way, it's a little glimpse of heaven! Of course, we are human and often fail, but sharing this common goal is enough to keep me going.

Leslie Wolf Robb
Director of Music Ministries
St. Paul's Lutheran Church and School, San Diego, California

I've been blessed to have the same church job for the past twenty-six years. During that time we have had only one change of pastoral leadership. My previous church position was for ten years, all with the same pastor. There are many commonalities in the working relationships I've had with these three pastors, but the following pertains to our current pastor and how we work together.

I feel that it is vital to have a good working relationship with the whole church staff, not just the pastor. We have a weekly church staff meeting that includes Bible study and prayer time, which helps to connect us as we share in each other's lives. We have a day school as well, and the entire staff gathers on Thursdays for prayer time and on Fridays for devotions. I appreciate the pastor's focus on building faith and relationships with the staff, as well as with the members of the congregation.

Spending non-working time with fellow staff members has helped build strong relationships, too. Quick trips to Starbucks, birthday lunches, staff parties, staff retreats, and service projects like working together on a Habitat for Humanity project or at Ronald McDonald House have made our relationships strong, or to use today's language, have made us a team.

It is understood that each of us brings various gifts to our ministry, and those are respected and acknowledged by everyone. All are willing to go above and beyond their job description when necessary. Mutual respect is strong!

One of the things that I have learned from our pastor is to really think about priorities. We all have things that matter to us for which we want to dig in our heels, but obviously no one person can have his or her own way all the time. The pastor's favorite phrase for things like this is "It's not a hill I'm going to die on." This has helped me to acquiesce on things that really weren't all that important and to save my passion and energy for those things that matter most to me. For example, the pastor is not fond of the terms "prelude" and "postlude" in the bulletin. He feels that in our beach community these words sound stilted and that some people won't understand them, and prefers to use "pre-service music" and "post-service music" instead. I don't like those at all, but have learned to save my energy for things that are more important to me and to our ministry. Give and take in working relationships is vital. The pastor's words would be, "Keep doing those things that make an *eternal* difference—that share Jesus."

Michael D. Boney
Canon for Music
St. Michael's Episcopal Cathedral, Boise, Idaho

For over twenty-five years I have been actively involved in the church and have had quite a plethora of experiences with clergy. At a very early age I felt a calling to ministry within the church. Being responsible for people's musical and spiritual development and enrichment is a very daunting yet rewarding call. In this call to music ministry, I am reminded that my work is not done alone but in relationship with others. The ability to work with clergy is essential to a healthy ministry but definitely comes with challenges for both musician and clergy.

After taking my current music position, I had an initial meeting with the senior clergyman during which we talked about his vision for the church and how my vision of the music ministry might be of support. He then shared something with me that I found comforting. He said he would never ask me to do anything that I was adamantly opposed to. This intrigued me because in all the churches I have worked in I had never had a clergy person say this to me. For the very first time in my career I felt that my education and experience was truly valued, and this has led to a good working relationship.

No relationship is without its struggles, but I have found that being able to disagree, agreeably and without malicious intent, can create an environment for mutual growth, both spiritually and collegially. It is easy to succumb solely to appreciating your ideas, your thoughts, and those who think as you do, but I find there really isn't any challenge involved in this type of mutuality. My work in the church goes beyond my own desires and passions and must encompass the needs of the congregation which I serve. Initially, whenever I was confronted with a request from my pastor regarding music or liturgy with which I did not necessarily agree, my response was one of frustration and opposition. This type of response became unhealthy and unfruitful for me, the pastor, and the congregation. After a period of time, I approached things differently and learned that I needed to be challenged beyond my comfort level. The congregation deserves to have music and liturgy that reflects its current understanding of aesthetics and theology. Moving forward, I have tried to replace personal aspirations with spiritual discernment and openness to God's call. It has greatly reduced my frustrations and allowed me to focus on ministry.

To this end, I believe two things must occur between clergy and musician in order to create an environment of mutual respect, spirituality, and growth. The clergy and musician must see each other as skilled in their respective vocations, and they must be open to change and challenge for the good of the congregation and glory of God. The relationship between clergy and musician is vital to the life and growth of any church. For either to possess an elitist attitude towards the other is destructive and repugnant to Christ's teachings. "Just as I have loved you, you also should love one another. By this everyone will know that you are my disciples, if you have love [and respect] for one another." (John 13: 34b–35. NRSV)

Name withheld
Organist-Choirmaster
Episcopal churches

I did not see it coming. Through many years of working as an organist–director, I had essentially lived in a little cocoon of love and appreciation, with collegial clergy friends and mostly pleasant choristers. I heard plenty of horror stories, and they saddened and sometimes angered me, but I could only think how blessed I had been. Then it happened to me.

It started with a transition from one pastor-and-mentor's retirement and progressed through an interim situation (while our excellent staff carried on) to the new pastor. What he did not know was that an important denominational officer had asked our small staff in this medium-sized church to stay intact for at least six months to aid in the transition. What we did not know was that the new pastor expected us all to offer our resignations. What we witnessed right away was the previously inclusive atmosphere morphing into a "my way or the highway" mentality. Regular office hours and meetings made way for the pastor's breezing in and out of the office, his inaccessibility, long hours on e-mail, criticism, arguments in meetings with lay people, a general degradation of atmosphere.

People began to leave. It was sad to lose beloved associates. There was a wonderful festival service at which the pastor stood up and gave a public airing, during his sermon, of our differences as he perceived them. I was dumbfounded! I think I was in full denial at that stage. Later I was ambushed into a staged confrontation in his office, at which I was told how "difficult" I am by two other people. When I got up to leave, I heard a family member's voice in an adjacent office, and as I stumbled toward the door, the pastor grabbed my arm and said (with an artificial grin on his face), "I am your boss, and I order you to smile!"

I had held on partly because the college at which I taught had no organ, and I was currently teaching two wonderful organ majors. Finally, I played a gig with a local chorus, spent the night cleaning out my office, and left my resignation (very professional in tone) under the pastor's door. One of the final indignities: he spread the word that I was "retiring." When I heard that, I made it clear: "I am not retiring; I quit."

My lack of awareness was epic. I also felt isolated, which I later learned is typical in abusive situations. I blamed myself, and I was fearful of being labeled a troublemaker. I was afraid I would never be hired again. I lost a good location, a desirable venue, and a place to teach. I feared possible damage to my reputation.

Lessons learned:

1. Have faith. Friends and colleagues called and offered me places to practice and teach. Many called just to inquire how I was doing.
2. Understand the dangers in transitions.
3. Keep up one's professional contacts and keep the resume current. Network; don't stay home. Don't be afraid to talk; just keep it on a professional level.
4. The healing process is very lengthy. One will never really be the same again.

I gained things I could never have gotten from all of the lovely situations combined. I gained rapport, empathy, and the ability to work effectively in situations where there were really wounded people. I learned to inspire and lead in healthy situations; how to reach out; how to communicate effectively, even in difficult conversations; and how to build a program. I know how to talk and listen to others who have been in abusive situations. I have learned forgiveness, and I have examined myself for the things that triggered such responses. Maybe I will never know, but I have definitely grown spiritually from the experience.

Carol Feather Martin
Director of Music and Arts, Organist
Trinity Presbyterian Church, Arlington, Virginia

My current employment situation is the best I have had in my thirty-four years of music ministry. I've previously worked with a pastor who did not use the lectionary, but only preached on his chosen personal and political topics. Initially, worship planning happened in the middle of the week before the Sunday service. After about five years, I was able to convince him to plan in advance so that my music would reflect the theme of the day. He eventually came to plan six months in advance. During the last few years before his retirement, he became disillusioned with ministry, put forth no effort, and became a bully.

Another pastor was removed for non-physical improprieties. He continually micromanaged our work and bullied and belittled the staff to other staff members and members of the congregation. He made inappropriate remarks about church members to other church members and laughed about it. This was all done in private and hidden for about six years before enough people found out what was going on and action was taken. Denominational officials became involved, and the congregation suffered financial stresses in order to have his contract terminated.

The current senior pastor was a music major with a degree in voice before she entered seminary. Not only does she have an appreciation of music, she sings whenever possible and gives total support to the staff in every way. We have weekly worship planning meetings which include the Worship and Music Committee Chair and a representative from the contemporary style service as well. Together we discuss the lectionary topics for services a month to six weeks in advance and choose liturgy and images for the bulletin and online publications. Our staff ministry is that of a team of professionals who support each other and do whatever needs to be done to care for the congregation and enliven worship and ministry. The congregation is very active with average attendance percentages at about fifty percent of membership. Although membership hovers around 500 in a transient area, there are many families with children who become involved early and remain connected.

Attributes with negative consequences

- Distrust
- Micromanagement
- Bullying
- Public comparison to other employees
- Gossip
- Verbal abuse
- Lack of early service preparation
- Lack of cooperation
- Extreme criticism

Attributes with positive effects

- Use of the lectionary and creative planning
- Worship planning team meetings
- Joint selection of hymns and service music
- Support for entire music program
- Entire staff works together as a team
- Complete trust to do my work
- Constructive review and critique

Marcia Van Oyen
Minister of Music, Worship and Fine Arts
Plymouth First United Methodist Church, Plymouth, Michigan

I embarked on my journey as a church musician armed with plenty of musical knowledge and skills, but it wasn't until I had been in the role for some years that I understood what being a church musician is really about. It's about being a vessel, a vessel that is filled by watching and listening and sensing and letting God in, and is poured out in service and sacrifice and celebration. It's about letting experiences and people shape you, broadening your perspective and invading your heart. It's about learning how to stay in step with other leaders in the dance of worship. It's about unselfconsciously offering your efforts to God and helping others to do that, too. It's about being a shepherd and a servant leader. It's about knowing that you would keep making music even if no one but God was there to hear it.

And it's about working with pastors. A productive relationship between pastor and musician is founded on honesty. Whether you and your pastor like each other or not, or agree on everything or not, the road to working together fruitfully is paved with direct and open communication. Find out what's important to your pastor, tell him or her what is important to you and what you need to do your job effectively. Clarify expectations—the pastor's for you and yours for the pastor. Show your pastor that you are someone she or he can trust and who won't sow seeds of dissension when the going gets rough. I've found that by using this approach, I grew to like the pastors to whom I was initially not drawn, and developed wonderful partnerships with those with whom I had an immediate rapport. I've certainly chosen less than optimal ways of communicating and have made unfair assumptions about non-musical pastors, and I've been disappointed by pastors who have made assumptions about me because I'm a musician with a doctorate. But when you can relate human to human, without labels and preconceived notions, the potential for a fruitful working relationship can be realized, and your whole church will benefit.

Name withheld
Organist and Choirmaster
Protestant churches

Our family was dedicated to participating in the life of our church. Both my parents were choir directors. With piano lessons at age five, I began preparing for a career in church music, although I did not realize it at the time. During my high school years, I served as church organist and then went on to college and earned a master of music degree.

In the years that followed, I came to appreciate the potential power of sacred music and wanted church music to be my life's work. As a professional, I studied and worked with choirs and congregations to create those moments of clarity and truth that can only come to us through music's unique, personal, and universal language. I believed that music in corporate worship was integral to our growth as Christians.

After forty years in service of the church, I came to realize that Christian charity and kindness can "go missing." I loved and received many blessings from my last position as music director and organist. Highlights included the institution of an AIDS Benefit Concert Series and yearly choir retreats. A few days after the last choir retreat I was called into the interim pastor's office. The day before, he had asked me for the name of a good organ substitute "just in case he had an occasion to call one." I should have been putting two and two together. There were just three people present—the interim pastor, the chair of the personnel committee, and me. After the chairwoman prayed that God would be with us, she told me they had to let me go. This came as a complete shock to me. There had been no warning, no discussion of any major problems, and no complaints to me about my work.

Although the interim pastor had met separately with all other staff members and visited them in their offices, he never made time for me, even when I offered to meet with him, and he hesitated to come into my office. He would stop at the door for any necessary conversation. I brought this up at the meeting. When confronted by the personnel chair, the pastor admitted that this was true. She looked at him with shock and frustration. But the meeting continued, and I was given two choices: Leave immediately with three months' severance pay or stay on for three months and pretend that I had chosen to leave at the end of that time. Meanwhile, I was not to discuss any portion of the real circumstances of my departure. In doing so I would be charged with insubordination, fired, and risk losing any severance.

The choir and congregation did not believe I had suddenly decided to leave. At first the interim pastor told them I had decided to retire. That explanation went nowhere. There was much anger. The personnel committee finally had to meet with an outraged and shocked choir. The pastor explained that it had been his job to carry out what would have been too difficult for the former pastor to do.

I was never given the opportunity to address any issues. There was no conversation as to what I could do to keep my job. At the time of my departure I was led to believe that I had no legal rights and was threatened by the interim pastor. In the final analysis, shouldn't we church musicians be able to expect that any difficulties, perceived or otherwise, be settled in a Christian manner? Shouldn't we expect to be treated with respect and honesty in the process? Isn't the church the perfect setting to practice our own Christianity?

I have moved on but cannot say that even after a few years I have fully recovered from the experience. My symptoms of post-traumatic stress disorder (diagnosed by my physician) have thankfully abated with time. It is like a death of a loved one. You learn to live with the loss. My faith as a Christian remains strong. Music has and will always be a huge blessing in my life. Not so sure about "church."

Gary Davison
Organist and Choirmaster
Saint Francis Episcopal Church, Potomac Parish, Potomac, Maryland

The Reverend William (Billy) M. Shand, III, and I first met in the early 1990s when I journeyed to Washington to interview for several church music job openings. Of the five positions for which I applied, four made an offer of immediate employment. The fifth, St. Francis Episcopal Church, had already extended an offer to another candidate but asked if I could delay any decisions until they had heard from that person. I obliged since it was my top choice given their rector but, not surprisingly, was soon informed the other musician had accepted. However, despite that turn of events, the stage was set for what has become a wonderfully long and fruitful working relationship with Mr. Shand.

In the meantime, I declined the other four offers for varying reasons and ended up in New York City in a lovely, small Anglo-Catholic parish with a dynamic and equally lovely rector with whom I happily have remained friends. But in late 1994, Mr. Shand called to inform me the full-time music position at St. Francis Church once again was open. When he asked if I was interested I had to admit I still was, but tentatively so. You see, I loved my little church on Manhattan's Upper East Side, and ... I recently was engaged to a fine soprano who would profit more from staying in Gotham. However, in my heart of hearts, I knew Mr. Shand and I would be a good match and this was, after all, a full-time job. My speculation on our compatibility was a just hunch, I suppose, but I sensed he and I had good chemistry and we seemed to have similar views on the important role of refined music in general and in the church specifically. (The conspicuous portrait of Handel over his desk was but one of the clues!) At any rate, he must have sensed the same thing and had stayed in touch even after my move to New York City. That was critical to me, and I have never forgotten it.

Seventeen years on now, I can say honestly the legs upon which our success stands are respect and trust. That may sound like a cliché, but it's true. We understand the hierarchy under which we operate and find no threat—nor seek any!—within it. There's absolutely no point in that. It's a good model and it works well, given respect and trust. Without a doubt, we truly do respect each other's role and the expertise we bring to them. After all, we both worked very hard to achieve a certain professional proficiency, and we maintain a course of continuing education and the nurturing of that delicate art called networking. The long-term benefits of both are very healthy for any parish on top of the gains for each individual.

Of no small consequence, Mr. Shand and I are very fortunate in that we both had excellent parental guidance in which a solid work ethic was fundamental and education highly valued. Even with all its foibles, church was *never* an option in our households and a Christian life ultimately was—and still is!—a worthy life. Because of that, in part, we trust each other implicitly to fulfill our obligations with consistently high standards, staying focused compassionately and intelligently on the church's raison d'être—worship. Beyond our basic trust in each other, we wholeheartedly trust that what we are doing is, indeed, "meet and right," part of a long succession of those intrepid stewards of the faith. Even in the midst of doubt and the shifting sands of our own fickle age, we still believe firmly that dignified Christian worship connected to our past and mindful of our future remains our present bounden duty. For me, to have the opportunity to adorn that sort of intention with beautiful, refined music—with enthusiastic support and encouragement, no less—is a blessing beyond measure. It has made all the difference for me and nurtured a most treasured partnership with Mr. Shand.

John Walker
Professor of Organ Performance
Peabody Institute, Baltimore, Maryland

During the autumn semester of my freshman year in high school, and just a few weeks after my first formal organ lesson, I was pressed into service one Sunday morning when the resident organist of our church became suddenly ill. For an entire month I continued to fulfill the real need of the church until the organist was able to return to her post.

Since my father was pastor of that congregation, I also sensed that I was participating in the ministerial role of our family. That opportunity initiated my self-identification as a church musician and close colleague of the pastor, a concept that has grown steadily clearer during fifty-six ensuing years in the ministry of music.

Counting my father as my first pastor, I have been privileged to serve with a total of twenty-five senior and interim ministers, many associate pastors, and several rabbis and cantors. I have grown to regard myself as fully ecumenical and as an experienced observer of clergy. Over these years so many pastors have left their deep imprint upon me. I hope that they remember me with a portion of the gratitude with which I recall them. Here is a short list of those pastors who have left an indelible mark on my life:

Dennis Nyberg, who, by suggesting that one can greatly expand a sphere of influence by effective delegation of responsibilities, convinced me of the worth of energy spent upon administration and the art of delegation.

Douglas Hayward, who taught me the art of "gentling people," effecting change by gentle means. Also, on the day of my father's death, Doug remained with my mother for many hours until I could be located, for which I have been forever grateful.

William Sloane Coffin, Jr. From my early days of awe I grew to know Bill as a treasured friend. Bill convinced me of the fullness of God's grace and the need for genuine faith to result in works. Bill Coffin was an accomplished pianist. The congregation and I were delighted when occasionally he would play the piano during the prelude to worship. One of his most memorable sermons was delivered from the piano, where he demonstrated most brilliantly the many possible resolutions of a diminished-seventh chord, comparing that chord to life with its infinite possibilities. At the conclusion of each service of worship, Bill would remain in place beside the organ console during the postlude, relishing the opportunity to be as close as possible to all music. Responding to his gesture, the congregation likewise remained for the postlude, after which Bill would greet everyone at the door.

James A. Forbes, Jr. In 1989, when Dr. Forbes became senior minister at The Riverside Church, he proclaimed a vision of multicultural maturity in which every service of worship would contain something (1) European/Eurocentric, (2) African/African American, (3) Hispanic, and (4) Asian. At that time, I sensed that I had repertoire for categories 1 and 2, but not much for categories 3 and 4. Stimulated by Dr. Forbes' vision, for the past two decades I have worked to expand my repertoire and the cultural vocabulary of my congregations' music. As a result of Dr. Forbes' vision in 1989, my choir at Brown Memorial Presbyterian Church in Baltimore now sings in Mandarin, Swahili, Old Church Slavonic, and frequently in English, Latin, French, German, and other European languages!

William Jackson, who taught me that change is inevitable although progress is optional.

Andrew Foster Connors. During the early months of 2004, Brown Memorial Park Avenue Presbyterian Church (Baltimore) concluded two independent searches for pastor and musician. The respective committees nominated Andrew Foster Connors as pastor and me, John Walker, as musician. Before accepting this position, Andrew and I first became acquainted with each other, thereby engaging each other in a covenantal relationship. With the blessing of both search committees, Andrew and I met by phone, and I immediately sensed a deep rapport with Andrew, a relationship of mutual trust and respect that continues to grow steadily until this day.

As the son of a Presbyterian pastor, I have always suspected that my call to music ministry resulted from my wish to follow in my father's path. Andrew somehow perceived my latent pastoral desire. Shortly after we both arrived in Baltimore, Andrew asked the church session to rename my position as minister of music. After several decades of full-time work in the church, I have been surprised and delighted to recognize my role in a fully new concept. This identity promotes my full and open engagement with Andrew and members of the congregation on many levels, thanks to the generosity of his spirit to welcome me into this collegial relationship.

Andrew has frequently expressed regret that he has not studied as much music as have I, thereby expressing his honor of my discipline! At the same time, I can readily say to Andrew that I have not studied as much theology as has he. By our mutual respect, not only do we continue to grow and to learn from each other, but our congregation also grows, learns, and develops steadily into a more harmonious community. The congregation will always mirror the relationships members inevitably perceive between clergy and musicians.

Believing the relationship between pastor and musician to be of paramount importance for health in the total ministry of the parish, we musicians and clergy must seek constantly to form and strengthen a ministerial partnership. In the synagogue we would be seen as rabbi and cantor. As sacred musicians, we have a high and noble calling to become ministers who bring our professional skills to strengthen the body of Christ, the Church.

Coda

I hope by now you share my conviction that a collegial relationship between clergy and musician is essential to creating meaningful worship and maximizing the potential for their ministry. This relationship needs to be one that is supportive, collegial, and respectful; honors each other's skills and gifts; and appreciates both person's strengths and weaknesses. It must be a relationship where each is thrilled for the other's success (not threatened by it), and that allows musicians to share their gifts of teaching and pastoral care, prayer, and vision.

The literature supporting the value and the effectiveness of teamwork is abundant. Michael Gorman, in his recent article "The Church Musician as (Overlooked) Theologian," (Duke, *Divinity* Magazine) points out that clergy and musicians both share a responsibility for the doxology of the church. Epperly and Hollinger in their book *From a Mustard Seed: Enlivening Worship and Music in the Small Congregation* further suggest that clergy and musicians can be friends, share common goals in ministry and worship, communicate well, understand each other's strengths and weaknesses, and respect each other's roles and unique gifts and nurture and support them.

Although musicians often have not been treated well, they have not always conducted themselves as they should. The playing field is not a level one. Yet how can we ignore the fact that we are created equal in God's sight and, as children of God, are called to live out that premise. Yes, each of us has different gifts, but each of us has talents and strengths and passions that, when used with integrity and for the greater good of God's creation, will enrich the church in ways we can scarcely imagine.

The question is not who is more important—you or I—but rather what we, as the people of God, are being called to do at this time and in this place. A prayerful and faithful response will bring us to the conclusion that we are not rivals, we are a team.

Bibliography

Are, Thomas L. *Faithsong: A New Look at the Ministry of Music.* Philadelphia: The Westminster Press, 1981.

Ballou, Hugh. *Creating and Sustaining Healthy Teams: Preventing and Managing Team Conflict.* Blacksburg: SynerVision International, Inc., 2011. [ebook]

———. *Moving Spirits, Building Lives: The Church Musician as Transformational Leader, ed.* Blacksburg: SynerVision International, Inc, 2005.

Bonhoeffer, Dietrich. *Life Together*, tr. Daniel W. Bloesch and James H. Burtness. Minneapolis: Fortress Press, 2004.

Bridges, William. *Transitions: Making Sense of Life's Changes.* Cambridge, MA: Perseus Books, 1980.

Coffin, William Sloane. *A Passion for the Possible: A Message to U.S. Churches,* 2nd ed. Louisville: Westminster/John Knox Press, 2004.

Coffman, James R. *Work and Peace in Academe: Leveraging Time, Money, and Intellectual Energy through Managing Conflict.* Bolton, MA: Anker Publishing Company, Inc., 2005.

Collins, James C. *Good to Great: Why Some Companies Make the Leap ... and Others Don't.* New York: HarperCollins, 2001.

Cooperrider, David L. and Diana Whitney. *Appreciative Inquiry: A Positive Revolution in Change.* San Francisco: Berrett-Koehler, 2005.

Ehrich, Thomas. *Church Wellness: A Best Practices Guide to Nurturing Healthy Congregations.* New York: Church Publishing Incorporated, 2008.

Episcopal Church. Regarding Music and Ministry (Canon II 6.1-4), *Constitution and Canons of The Episcopal Church.* New York: Church Publishing Incorporated, 2006.

Epperly, Bruce G. and Daryl Hollinger. *From a Mustard Seed: Enlivening Worship and Music in the Small Church.* Bethesda, MD: The Alban Institute, 2010.

Gorman, Michael. "The Church Musician as (Overlooked) Theologian," *Divinity* Magazine 11, no.1 (2011).

Greenleaf, Robert K. *Servant Leadership: A Journey into the Nature of Legitimate Power and Greatness.* New York: Paulist Press, 1977.

Hickman, Hoyt L., ed. *The Faith We Sing.* Nashville: Abingdon Press, 2000.

Johnson, Spencer. *Who Moved My Cheese? An Amazing Way To Deal With Change In Your Work And In Your Life.* New York: G. P. Putnam's Sons, 1998.

Katzenbach, Jon R. and Douglas K. Smith. "The Discipline of Teams," *Harvard Business Review* 83, no. 7/8 (July-August 2005): 162-171.

Koch, Ruth N. and Kenneth C. Haugt. *Speaking the Truth in Love: How to be an Assertive Christian.* St. Louis: Stephen Ministries, 1992.

Kroeker, Charlotte. *The Sounds of our Offerings: Achieving Excellence in Church Music.* Herndon, VA: Alban Institute, 2011.

Larson, Carl E. and Frank M. J. LaFasto. *Teamwork: What Must Go Right/ What Can Go Wrong.* Newbury Park, CA: SAGE Publications, 1989.

Lawson, Kevin E. *How to Thrive in Associate Staff Ministry.* Bethesda, MD: Alban Institute, 2000.

Lencioni, Patrick. *The Five Dysfunctions of a Team: A Leadership Fable.* San Francisco: Jossey-Bass, 2002.

Long, Thomas G. *Beyond the Worship Wars: Building Vital and Faithful Worship.* Herndon, VA: Alban Institute, 2001.

Maxwell, John C. *Teamwork 101: What Every Leader Needs to Know.* Nashville: Thomas Nelson, 2008.

———. *The 17 Essential Qualities of a Team Player: Becoming the Kind of Person Every Team Wants.* Nashville: Thomas Nelson, 2002.

Moores, David R. "Clergy-Organist Relationships," *The American Organist* 19, no. 8 (1985): 46-47.

Nouwen, Henri J. M. *Out of Solitude: Three Meditations on the Christian Life.* Notre Dame, IN: Ave Maria Press, 2004.

Orr, N. Lee. *The Church Music Handbook for Pastors and Musicians.* Nashville: Abingdon Press, 1991.

Parks, Lewis A. and Bruce C. Birch. *Ducking Spears, Dancing Madly: A Biblical Model of Church Leadership.* Nashville: Abingdon Press, 2004.

Presbyterian Church (USA). Pastor and Choir Director [W-1.4005b], *The Constitution of the Presbyterian Church (USA), Part II: Book of Order, 2009-2011.* Louisville: The Office of the General Assembly, 2009.

Roberts, William Bradley. *Music and Vital Congregations: A Practical Guide for Clergy.* New York: Church Publishing Incorporated, 2009.

Rupp, Joyce. *The Cup of our Life: A Guide for Spiritual Growth.* Notre Dame, IN: Ave Maria Press, 1997.

Setser, John K. *Broken Hearts, Shattered Trust: Workplace Abuse of Staff in the Church.* [n.p.], 2006.

Sirota, Victoria. *Preaching to the Choir: Claiming the Role of Sacred Musician.* New York: Church Publishing Incorporated. 2006.

Sitkin, Sim B. and J. Richard Hackman. "Developing Team Leadership: An Interview with Coach Mike Krzyzewski," *Academy of Management Learning and Education* 10, no. 3 (2011): 494-501.

Stone, Douglas, Bruce Patton, and Sheila Heden. *Difficult Conversations: How to Discuss What Matters Most.* New York: Penguin Books, 1999.

Weems, Lovett H., Jr. *Church Leadership: Vision, Team, Culture, and Integrity,* Rev. ed. Nashville: Abingdon Press, 2010.

Weiser, Conrad W. *Healers: Harmed and Harmful.* Minneapolis: Augsburg Fortress, 1994.

Westermeyer, Paul. *The Church Musician,* Rev. ed. Minneapolis: Augsburg Fortress, 1997.

Index